Southern Living.

The SOUTHERN HERITAGE COOKBOOK LIBRARY

The SOUTHERN HERITAGE
Sea
and
Stream
COOKBOOK

OXMOOR HOUSE
Birmingham, Alabama

Southern Living ®

The Southern Heritage Cookbook Library

Library of Congress Catalog Number: 84-61240
ISBN: 0-8487-0612-9

Manufactured in the United States of America

The Southern Heritage SEA AND STREAM Cookbook

Manager, Editorial Projects: Ann H. Harvey
Southern Living® *Foods Editor*: Jean W. Liles
Production Editor: Joan E. Denman
Foods Editor: Katherine M. Eakin
Assistant Foods Editor: Lynne B. Otwell
Director, Test Kitchen: Laura N. Massey
Test Kitchen Home Economists: Kay E. Clarke, Rebecca J. Riddle, Elizabeth J. Taliaferro, Dee Waller, Elise Wright Walker
Production Manager: Jerry R. Higdon
Copy Editor: Melinda E. West
Editorial Assistants: Patty E. Howdon, Mary Ann Laurens, Karen P. Traccarella
Food Photographer: Jim Bathie
Food Stylist: Sara Jane Ball
Layout Designer: Christian von Rosenvinge
Mechanical Artist: Faith Nance
Research Editors: Evelyn deFrees, Alicia Hathaway

Special Consultants

Art Director: Irwin Glusker
Heritage Consultant: Meryle Evans
Foods Writer: Lillian B. Marshall
Food and Recipe Consultants: Marilyn Wyrick Ingram, Audrey P. Stehle

Cover: The plate of Daphne Lodge Fried Catfish and Hush Puppies (page 110) is surrounded by fruits of the sea (clockwise): Red Snapper, Oysters, Clams, Boiled Shrimp (page 46), and Steamed Blue Crabs (page 17). Seafood Cocktail Sauce (page 126) will complement each one. Photograph by Jim Bathie.

CONTENTS

INTRODUCTION

The story of fish and shellfish in the South is a long and sometimes painful one. It began with an astonishing abundance of high protein ocean and fresh water food, scorned by a hungry group of transplanted Englishmen. There followed nearly a century of slow realization of its value, which culminated in the region's current love affair with what is left of our edible marine life. This book brings into focus the ways in which the South made delicious peace with the fruits of sea and stream.

When John Smith bought into the Virginia Company and set sail for America, he was not unaware of the conditions to be found here. Over a period of centuries, a body of lore had accumulated in Europe about America. The Vikings, operating out of Iceland and Greenland, had been using the rich North American fishing grounds since before the year 1000. When Columbus landed his first voyage hundreds of miles to the south in the 1400s, his famished crew gratefully wolfed down, without even cooking them, oysters, fish, and conchs.

Smith knew that Europeans had explored, conquered, pirated, and slaved along the Southeastern shores for years and that Sir Walter Raleigh had sent an expedition to stake out Virginia for England in 1584.

Yet, despite all the fish stories he must have heard, it was with awe that he wrote of " . . . fish, lying so thicke with their heads above the water, as for want of nets . . . we attempted to catch them with a frying pan . . . neither better fish, more plentie, nor more varietie for small fish, had any of us seen in any place. . . . " As ebbing tides left windrows of lobsters on Northern beaches, oysters over a foot long were not uncommon along the Southeast coast. Tidal pools were alive with crab. And, as the white man found when he penetrated inland, nature had blessed the fresh water as richly as the salt to man's advantage.

For many reasons, the Southerner did not recognize the "gold" in the "South Sea" on which he lived. Oyster roasts and fish fries did not come into vogue until around 1700. By that time, pork was the prime meat dish; the Southerner came to appreciate his fish and shellfish after his desperate need for it had passed, and then made up for lost time by building an unsurpassed cuisine around it.

SHELLFISH DELICACIES

As the Southern states matured, they evolved culinary personalities, much as children of a large family remain a little alike while becoming different. Each state with a coastline had put its mark on shellfish cookery well before the Civil War, with variations dictated largely by the ethnic background of those actually doing the cooking. A wide gulf existed between food in the homes of the well-to-do and those of the poor. And there was a gap between home cooking and food served in Southern hostelries. Northern travelers like Frederick Law Olmstead, the landscape architect, wrote scurrilous reviews of public eateries in the South.

Maryland and Virginia perfected she-crab soup, served shrimp for breakfast, and frolicked on the beaches with oyster roasts. Politicians recognized opportunity on sight: Many a candidacy has been announced to sated captives at an oyster roast. Steamed Blue Crab was popular all down the coast for outdoor parties as well, shells falling where they might.

North Carolina, settled later, caught the shellfish spirit from its neighbors. Charleston and Savannah were centers of a special blend of talents. Huguenot and African cooks, supplied with West Indian imports, combined tiny native shrimp with harvests from Low Country rice fields to make pilau or "perloo," characteristic of the region.

Florida has it all, goes the saying, plus stone crab. Rarely obtainable outside Florida, meat from stone crab claws, the only part eaten, is famous for its delicacy of flavor. The waters surrounding Florida and Key West also yield conch for chowder and fritters as well as a saltwater crayfish called rock or spiny lobster, of which only the tail meat is eaten.

A pleasant culture shock occurs every time a visitor first confronts Louisiana's Creole and Cajun shellfish. Choose between the urbane French-Spanish Creole style of New Orleans, where Africans brought okra for gumbo, and the earthier, country French-Acadian alchemy west of New Orleans, where Choctaws added filé powder to that gumbo.

The Southeast United States came gift-wrapped in delicious shellfish.

A shellfish feast on the dock at Severn Inn, Annapolis, Maryland: Steamed Blue Crabs, Steamed Clams, corn-on-the-cob; melted butter, condiments, and beer standing by. Mallet and knife are welcome tools at a crab fest.

C L A M S

STEAMED CLAMS

3 dozen cherrystone clams
  in shells
1 tablespoon seafood
  seasoning
1 tablespoon salt
1 teaspoon pepper
½ cup water
¼ cup butter or margarine,
  melted

Wash clams thoroughly, discarding any shells that have opened. Place clams in a large Dutch oven, and sprinkle with seafood seasoning, salt, and pepper. Add water; bring to a boil. Cover; reduce heat, and steam 10 minutes or until shells open wide. Remove clams from Dutch oven; drain, reserving liquid. Strain liquid.

Serve clams hot in shells with separate containers of clam liquid and melted butter. Yield: 3 servings or 6 appetizer servings.

CLAMS CASINO

1 dozen cherrystone clams
  in shells
¼ teaspoon Worcestershire
  sauce
¼ teaspoon hot sauce
3 slices bacon, cut into
  fourths
2 tablespoons Italian
  seasoned breadcrumbs

Wash clams, discarding any open (dead) clams. Pry open shells; discard top shell, and loosen meat from bottom shell. Arrange shells in a shallow baking pan.

Combine sauces, stirring well; brush clams lightly with sauce mixture. Top each with bacon, and sprinkle with breadcrumbs. Broil 4 inches from heating element 2 minutes or until edges of clams curl and bacon is done. Serve hot as an appetizer. Yield: 1 dozen.

Clams Casino, piquantly flavored and topped with bacon, make a stellar attraction at a party.

FRIED CHESAPEAKE BAY SOFT-SHELL CLAMS

1 quart soft-shell clams,
  shucked and drained
2 cups commercial pancake
  mix
Vegetable oil
Salt
Cocktail sauce (page 126)

Combine clams and 2 cups pancake mix in a medium mixing bowl; toss lightly until clams are well coated. Fry in deep hot oil (375°) for 2 minutes or until clams float to the top and are golden brown. Drain clams well on paper towels, and sprinkle with salt.

Transfer clams to a warm serving platter; serve immediately with cocktail sauce. Yield: 4 dozen.

An 1893 recipe booklet for Doxsee's Little Neck Clam Juice.

CLAM FRITTERS

¾ cup all-purpose flour
1½ teaspoons baking
  powder
¼ teaspoon salt
1 egg, lightly beaten
½ cup milk
1½ teaspoons shortening,
  melted
1 cup clams, drained and
  finely chopped
Vegetable oil
Cocktail sauce or tartar sauce
  (page 126)

Combine flour, baking powder, and salt in a medium mixing bowl; stir well, and set mixture aside.

Combine egg, milk, and shortening in a small mixing bowl; mix well, and stir into dry ingredients. Add clams; stir until smooth.

Drop clam mixture by tablespoonfuls into deep hot oil (375°); cook 3 minutes or until fritters float to the top and are golden brown. Drain well on paper towels.

Transfer fritters to a warm serving platter. Serve immediately with cocktail sauce or tartar sauce. Yield: 3 dozen.

LINGUINE WITH WHITE CLAM SAUCE

2 teaspoons sliced garlic
⅓ cup olive oil
2 (6½-ounce) cans minced
  clams, undrained
3 tablespoons finely chopped
  fresh parsley
½ (12-ounce) package
  linguine
1 tablespoon butter or
  margarine, melted
¼ teaspoon salt
¼ teaspoon pepper
2 tablespoons Chablis or
  other dry white wine
Grated Parmesan cheese

Sauté garlic in oil in a skillet over medium heat 2 minutes or until golden brown; remove garlic, and discard. Add clams to oil; cook 10 minutes over medium heat, stirring frequently. Stir in parsley; remove from heat. Set aside.

Cook linguine according to package directions; drain. Combine linguine and melted butter; stir well. Transfer linguine to a serving platter; set aside, and keep warm.

Bring clam mixture to a boil. Stir in salt, pepper, and wine. Remove from heat immediately. Pour sauce over linguine. Sprinkle with cheese, and serve immediately. Yield: 2 servings.

Atlantic Coast Indians originated the clambake, a seashore picnic which is still popular. They piled clams onto hot stones set in the ground where a fire had burned and gone out. The logistics are similar today, but we add things like corn-on-the-cob and potatoes. To those Indians, the clambake paid off, not only gastronomically but financially. They made beads and discs of clamshell; "wampum," not the Englishman's gold, meant money. The colonists were forced into a "clamshell economy."

CLAM CHOWDER

2 medium potatoes
2 slices bacon
½ cup chopped onion
4 (6½-ounce) cans minced
  clams, undrained
¼ cup butter or margarine
½ cup flour
1 quart milk
1 tablespoon Worcestershire
  sauce
½ teaspoon pepper
1 cup half-and-half

Scrub potatoes; cook in boiling water 25 minutes or until tender. Drain and cool slightly. Peel potatoes, and cut into ¾-inch cubes; set aside.

Cook bacon in a large skillet until crisp; remove bacon, reserving drippings in skillet.

Crumble bacon, and set aside.

Sauté onion in pan drippings until tender. Stir in clams; simmer 5 minutes.

Melt butter in a large saucepan over low heat; add flour, stirring until smooth. Cook 1 minute, stirring constantly. Gradually add milk; cook over medium heat, stirring constantly, until thickened and bubbly. Reduce heat; add potatoes, bacon, clam mixture, Worcestershire sauce, and pepper, stirring well. Slowly add half-and-half, stirring constantly. Cook over low heat until thoroughly heated, stirring frequently. Spoon into individual serving bowls; serve immediately. Yield: 2 quarts.

The quahog clam of Cape Cod ranges all the way to Florida, with some name changes along the way. Round clam or hard clam or quahog, the young ones are called cherrystones or, to use the Southern term, little necks. The long-neck clam in the Chesapeake Bay area is known locally as manninose (man-no), while in Virginia it may be called butterfish. The South votes with New England on chowder, though, preferring the milk-based variety over Manhattan-style.

Engraving of a chowder party, Harper's Weekly, *August, 1873.*

CONCH

FRIED CONCH

1 pound cleaned, skinned
  conch meat
2 eggs, lightly beaten
1 cup all-purpose flour
½ cup cornmeal
2 teaspoons salt
2 teaspoons pepper
Vegetable oil
Cocktail sauce (page 126)

Pound conch to ⅛-inch thickness, using a meat mallet or a rolling pin; cut into 1-inch pieces. Combine conch and eggs in a large mixing bowl; soak 2 to 3 minutes.

Combine flour, cornmeal, salt, and pepper in a large mixing bowl. Dredge conch in flour mixture until well coated. Carefully drop conch into deep hot oil (350°). Cook 3 minutes or until conch float to the top and are golden brown. Drain well on paper towels.

Transfer conch to a warm serving platter; serve with cocktail sauce. Yield: 4 servings.

CONCH FRITTERS

½ pound cleaned, skinned
  conch meat
⅔ cup all-purpose flour
1 teaspoon baking powder
½ teaspoon salt
¼ teaspoon pepper
3 tablespoons milk
1 egg, lightly beaten
1 tablespoon butter or
  margarine, melted
Vegetable oil
Cocktail sauce (page 126)

Grind conch meat using coarse blade of a meat grinder; set aside.

Combine flour, baking powder, salt, and pepper in a medium mixing bowl. Add milk, egg, and butter, mixing well. Stir in ground conch.

Drop batter by tablespoonfuls into deep hot oil (375°). Cook 2 minutes or until conch fritters float to the top and are golden brown. Drain on paper towels.

Transfer fritters to a warm serving platter, and serve with cocktail sauce. Yield: about 1½ dozen.

CONCH STEW

½ pound cleaned, skinned
  conch meat
1 small onion, chopped
3 tablespoons vegetable oil
2 tablespoons all-purpose
  flour
2 cups water
2 medium potatoes, peeled
  and cubed
½ teaspoon salt
¼ teaspoon pepper

Pound conch to ⅛-inch thickness, using a meat mallet or rolling pin. Cut conch into bite-size pieces; set aside.

Sauté onion in oil in a medium saucepan until tender; add flour, stirring well. Cook over medium heat, stirring frequently, until browned.

Add conch, water, potatoes, salt, and pepper; stir until well blended. Cook over medium heat, stirring frequently, until potatoes are tender. Serve immediately. Yield: about 1 quart.

KEY WEST CONCH CHOWDER

1½ pounds cleaned, skinned
  conch meat
¼ pound salt pork, diced
1 cup chopped onion
⅓ cup chopped green pepper
1 clove garlic, minced
3 cups water
1 (14½-ounce) can tomatoes,
  undrained and chopped
2 cups diced raw potatoes
2 bay leaves
1 (5.33-ounce) can evaporated
  milk
1 teaspoon salt
½ teaspoon pepper

Grind conch meat using coarse blade of a meat grinder; set aside.

Cook salt pork in a large Dutch oven until crisp; remove salt pork, reserving drippings in Dutch oven. Crumble salt pork, and set aside.

Sauté onion, green pepper, and garlic in drippings until tender.

Add ground conch, water, tomatoes, potatoes, and bay leaves to vegetable mixture. Bring to a boil. Reduce heat; cover and simmer 1 hour.

Add milk, salt, and pepper. Cook until thoroughly heated. (Do not boil.) Remove and discard bay leaves. Spoon chowder into individual serving bowls, and garnish with reserved salt pork. Serve immediately. Yield: 2 quarts.

C R A B

BROILED SOFT-SHELL CRABS

½ cup butter, melted and divided
3 tablespoons lemon juice
1 teaspoon salt, divided
½ teaspoon pepper, divided
8 dressed soft-shell crabs
1 tablespoon water
Chopped fresh parsley

Combine ¼ cup melted butter, lemon juice, ½ teaspoon salt, and ¼ teaspoon pepper in a small mixing bowl; stir well, and set aside.

Place crabs, back side up, in a shallow baking pan; sprinkle with remaining salt and pepper. Add water and remaining ¼ cup melted butter to pan.

Broil crabs 4 inches from heating element 3 minutes on each side or until crabs are lightly browned and crab legs are crisp.

Transfer crabs to a warm serving platter. Garnish with parsley, and serve with reserved butter sauce. Yield: 4 servings.

W hile most seafood enthusiasts never met a crab they didn't like, they reserve a special craving for it at the time it sheds its shell. At this moment, the "buster" is at its fattest and most succulent, to be eaten before the new shell starts to harden. From this stage, the shell stiffens to "paper shell," then back to hard shell.

SAUTÉED SOFT-SHELL CRABS

½ cup all-purpose flour
1 teaspoon salt
½ teaspoon pepper
8 dressed soft-shell crabs
½ cup butter, divided
3 tablespoons vegetable oil
2 tablespoons chopped fresh parsley
Juice of 1 lemon

Combine flour, salt, and pepper in a small mixing bowl; mix well. Dredge crabs in flour mixture, shaking off excess flour.

Melt ¼ cup butter in a large skillet over low heat; add oil, stirring well. Add dredged crabs, and sauté 5 minutes or until lightly browned, turning once. Remove crabs from skillet, and keep warm. Reserve butter mixture in skillet.

Add remaining butter to skillet, scraping bottom of pan to loosen sediment. Stir in parsley and lemon juice; cook over low heat until butter melts and sauce is thoroughly heated.

Arrange crabs on a serving platter; pour sauce over crabs, and serve immediately. Yield: 4 servings.

FRIED SOFT-SHELL CRABS

8 dressed soft-shell crabs
1 cup all-purpose flour
½ teaspoon salt
1 egg, lightly beaten
1 cup milk
Vegetable oil

Rinse crabs carefully; pat dry. Combine flour and salt; set aside. Combine egg and milk; beat well.

Dredge crabs in flour. Dip coated crabs into milk mixture; dredge again in flour.

Fry crabs in deep hot oil (370°) until golden brown; drain on paper towels. Serve immediately. Yield: 4 servings.

GRILLED SOFT-SHELL CRABS

1 cup vegetable oil
2 tablespoons vinegar
1 teaspoon lemon juice
1 teaspoon salt
1 teaspoon lemon pepper
¼ teaspoon dried whole tarragon
⅛ teaspoon garlic powder
12 dressed soft-shell crabs

Combine oil, vinegar, lemon juice, salt, lemon pepper, tarragon, and garlic powder; stir until well blended. Cover and refrigerate overnight.

Position crabs securely in a wire grilling basket. Place crabs, back side down, 4 inches from hot coals. Grill 10 minutes, basting frequently with sauce. Turn basket with crabs, and grill an additional 5 minutes. Baste frequently with remaining sauce. Serve immediately. Yield: 6 servings.

BUSTERS BÉARNAISE

1 cup milk
1 egg, lightly beaten
8 dressed soft-shell crabs
All-purpose flour
½ cup butter
Toast points
Béarnaise Sauce
Chopped fresh parsley
    (optional)

Combine milk and egg in a bowl. Dip each crab in milk mixture; dredge in flour.

Melt butter in a large skillet over low heat; add coated crabs, and cook until crabs are golden brown, turning once. Remove from heat; place crabs over toast points on a serving platter, and drizzle with Béarnaise Sauce. Sprinkle with parsley, if desired. Serve immediately. Yield: 4 servings.

Béarnaise Sauce:

¼ cup Chablis or other dry
    white wine
2 tablespoons tarragon
    vinegar
1 tablespoon chopped onion
⅛ teaspoon salt
⅛ teaspoon white pepper
1 tablespoon chopped fresh
    parsley
¾ cup butter, cut into small
    pieces and softened
3 egg yolks, lightly beaten

Combine wine, vinegar, onion, salt, pepper, and parsley in a heavy saucepan; cook over high heat, stirring occasionally, until mixture is reduced to 1½ tablespoons.

Reduce heat to low; add butter and yolks alternately, beginning and ending with butter. Whisk constantly until butter melts and mixture is smooth and thickened. Serve immediately. Yield: about 1 cup.

Young fisherman gingerly displays his catch for a photographer while another camera captures the scene. Pensacola, Florida, c.1915.

HOW TO CRACK INTO A CRAB

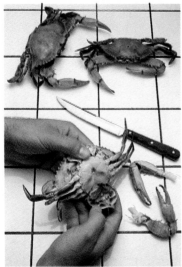

Step 1 — Remove the two large pincer claws by breaking off at the body. Set claws aside. Turn crab over; pry off apron flap, and discard.

Step 2 — Holding the crab in one hand, lift off the top of the shell. Using a knife, scrape out internal organs, and discard.

Step 3 — With a knife, make a straight cut from the back to the front of each side of the crab just above the leg joints. Make this cut deep enough to loosen the meat. Remove the meat.

Step 4 — Cut off the remaining legs where they join the body. Locate where the flat, paddle-shaped swim fins (backfin) attach to the body. Using a pick or knife point, carefully remove the large chunks of white muscle from either side of the crab. This is called backfin or lump crabmeat.

Step 5 — Using a pick or knife point, carefully pick through the cartilage to remove the remaining crabmeat from the chambers. This meat is referred to as flake or regular meat. Discard all cartilage.

Step 6 — With a sharp knife, cut through the shell of the claw just below the pincer. Gently break the shell open, and remove the claw meat.

STEAMED BLUE CRABS

½ cup seafood seasoning
½ cup salt
3 cups vinegar
3 cups flat beer
3 dozen live blue crabs

Combine seasonings, vinegar, and beer in a large mixing bowl; stir well.

Place 18 crabs on a rack in a very large stockpot with a tight fitting lid. Pour half of vinegar mixture over crabs. Repeat procedure with remaining crabs and vinegar mixture; cover stockpot with lid.

Place stockpot over high heat, and steam 20 minutes or until crabs turn bright red in color. Remove crabs immediately to a serving platter or bring crabs to room temperature, and refrigerate until ready to use. Yield: 3 dozen.

O f the many species of crab inhabiting the East coast waters, blue crab is the most plentiful, ranking behind lobster and shrimp in commercial value. The crab most often found on the menu at beach picnics, it is available from February, when the water turns warm around Florida, until cold weather returns. The stone crab, by contrast, is rare and expensive. Concentrated around Key West and Miami, it ranges up to the Carolinas and west to Texas. Only the claw meat is eaten; trappers break off one claw, and the crab regenerates a new one.

CRAB NORFOLK

½ cup butter
1 pound lump crabmeat
½ teaspoon salt
¼ teaspoon pepper
Juice of 1 lemon
½ cup chopped fresh parsley
Crusty French bread

Melt butter in a heavy skillet over low heat; add crabmeat, salt, and pepper. Sauté gently, being careful not to shred lump crabmeat. Add lemon juice and parsley; continue cooking until thoroughly heated. Remove from heat.

Spoon crabmeat mixture into four 6-ounce custard cups or ramekins. Serve with crusty bread pieces for dunking. Yield: 4 servings.

Commercial Place on a busy day in 1912, Norfolk, Virginia.

Crabbing at Port of Pensacola, Florida, c.1905.

CRAB IMPERIAL

1 tablespoon butter or
  margarine
1 tablespoon all-purpose flour
½ cup milk
1½ teaspoons Worcestershire
  sauce
1 teaspoon instant minced
  onion
2 slices bread, crusts
  removed and cubed
½ cup mayonnaise
1 tablespoon lemon juice
½ teaspoon salt
Pinch of pepper
1 pound lump crabmeat
¼ cup butter or margarine
Paprika

Melt 1 tablespoon butter in a heavy saucepan over low heat; add flour, stirring until smooth. Cook 1 minute, stirring constantly. Gradually add milk; cook over medium heat, stirring constantly, until thickened and bubbly. Stir in Worcestershire sauce and onion. Fold in bread cubes. Cool slightly. Stir in mayonnaise, lemon juice, salt, and pepper. Set aside.

Sauté crabmeat in ¼ cup butter in a heavy skillet. Stir into sauce. Spoon mixture into a lightly greased 1-quart casserole. Sprinkle paprika over top. Bake at 450° for 10 minutes or until hot and bubbly. Serve immediately. Yield: 4 servings.

COMMANDER'S PALACE CRABMEAT IMPERIAL

1 medium-size green pepper,
  diced
1½ cups mayonnaise, divided
2 eggs, lightly beaten
1 tablespoon English
  mustard
2 whole pimientos, drained
  and diced
1 teaspoon salt
½ teaspoon white pepper
3 pounds lump crabmeat
Paprika

Combine green pepper, 1 cup mayonnaise, eggs, mustard, pimiento, salt, and pepper in a large mixing bowl; mix well. Add crabmeat; mix gently so that lumps are not broken.

Place 8 crab shells or 6-ounce custard cups on a 15- x 10- x 1-inch jellyroll pan. Spoon 1 cup crabmeat mixture into each shell. Top evenly with remaining mayonnaise; sprinkle with paprika. Bake at 350° for 15 minutes. Serve hot or chilled. Yield: 8 servings.

CRABMEAT AU GRATIN

1 cup lump or flake crabmeat,
  drained
2 green onions, chopped
1 tablespoon butter or
  margarine
½ cup butter
4 egg yolks, lightly beaten
2 teaspoons lemon juice
½ teaspoon salt
¼ teaspoon white pepper
Grated Parmesan cheese

Sauté crabmeat and onion in 1 tablespoon butter until crabmeat is heated and onion is tender; set aside.

Melt ½ cup butter in top of a double boiler over boiling water. Gradually add yolks, stirring constantly, until slightly thickened. Stir in lemon juice, salt, and pepper. Fold reserved crabmeat-onion mixture into sauce.

Spoon mixture into four 6-ounce custard cups; sprinkle with cheese. Bake at 375° for 10 minutes or until lightly browned. Serve immediately. Yield: 4 servings.

BAKED CRAB IN SHELLS

1 pound lump or flake
  crabmeat, drained
1 small green pepper, finely
  chopped
2 tablespoons chopped
  fresh parsley
½ cup chopped onion
1 cup finely chopped celery
4 hard-cooked eggs,
  chopped
1 tablespoon Worcestershire
  sauce
3 tablespoons butter or
  margarine
¼ cup all-purpose flour
¼ teaspoon salt
1 cup milk
8 slices bread, toasted and
  crushed
1 cup mayonnaise

Combine first 7 ingredients in a large mixing bowl; mix well, and set aside.

Melt butter in a heavy saucepan over low heat; add flour and salt, stirring until smooth. Cook 1 minute, stirring constantly. Gradually add 1 cup milk; cook over medium heat, stirring constantly, until mixture is thickened and bubbly. Remove sauce from heat.

Spoon sauce into crabmeat mixture, mixing well. Add toast crumbs, reserving ¼ cup; mix well. Stir in mayonnaise.

Fill 12 crab shells or 6-ounce custard cups with crabmeat mixture; sprinkle reserved toast crumbs on top. Bake at 400° for 20 minutes. Serve immediately. Yield: 12 servings.

Bake something festive: Baked Crab in Shells (front) or Deviled Crab (page 20) in baking shells.

CRABMEAT SOUFFLÉ

3 tablespoons butter or
  margarine
3 tablespoons all-purpose
  flour
1 cup half-and-half
4 eggs, separated
¾ teaspoon dry mustard
½ teaspoon salt
⅛ teaspoon red pepper
1 pound lump or flake
  crabmeat, drained
2 teaspoons lime juice
¼ teaspoon cream of tartar

Melt butter in a large heavy saucepan over low heat; add flour, stirring until smooth. Cook 1 minute, stirring constantly. Gradually add half-and-half; cook over medium heat, stirring constantly, until thickened and bubbly. Remove from heat. Set aside.

Beat egg yolks until thick and lemon colored. Gradually stir one-fourth of hot white sauce mixture into yolks; add to remaining hot white sauce, stirring well. Stir in mustard, salt, and pepper.

Combine crabmeat and lime juice; stir crabmeat mixture into white sauce.

Beat egg whites (at room temperature) until foamy; add cream of tartar, beating until egg whites are stiff but not dry. Gently fold into hot crabmeat mixture.

Butter the bottom of a 1½-quart soufflé dish; pour crabmeat mixture into dish. Place dish in a large pan; add hot water to pan to a depth of 1 inch. Bake at 325° for 1 hour and 15 minutes or until puffed and golden brown. Serve hot. Yield: 6 servings.

DEVILED CRAB

½ cup cracker crumbs
1½ tablespoons butter or
  margarine, melted
½ pound claw crabmeat,
  drained and flaked
¼ cup mayonnaise, divided
2 tablespoons white wine
1 tablespoon Worcestershire
  sauce
1 tablespoon Dijon mustard
1 hard-cooked egg, chopped
¼ teaspoon hot sauce
¼ teaspoon ground nutmeg
¼ teaspoon paprika

Combine cracker crumbs and butter in a large mixing bowl; toss lightly. Add crabmeat, 3 tablespoons mayonnaise, wine, Worcestershire sauce, mustard, egg, hot sauce, and nutmeg; stir well. Spoon crabmeat mixture into 4 baking shells or 6-ounce custard cups. Top evenly with remaining mayonnaise; sprinkle with paprika.

Bake at 350° for 15 minutes; place crab shells 4 inches from heating element, and broil 2 minutes or until lightly browned. Yield: 4 servings.

Fritz Gaido poses beneath the giant crab sculpture atop his Houston eatery.

CHESAPEAKE HOUSE CRAB CAKES

1 egg, well beaten
2 tablespoons mayonnaise
1 tablespoon prepared
  mustard
1 tablespoon butter or
  margarine, melted
1 teaspoon chopped fresh
  parsley
½ teaspoon dry mustard
½ teaspoon seafood
  seasoning
½ teaspoon salt
¼ teaspoon pepper
1 pound claw crabmeat,
  drained and flaked
1½ cups soft breadcrumbs
Vegetable oil
Tartar sauce (page 126)

Combine egg, mayonnaise, prepared mustard, butter, parsley, dry mustard, seafood seasoning, salt, and pepper in a large mixing bowl; blend well. Gently fold in crabmeat.

Shape mixture into 8 patties; roll each in breadcrumbs. Fry in deep hot oil (350°) until crab cakes are brown and float to the top. Drain on paper towels.

Transfer crab cakes to a warm serving platter. Serve immediately with tartar sauce. Yield: 4 servings.

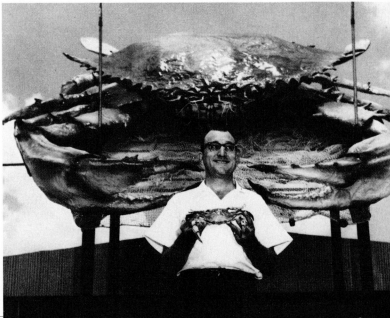

YBOR CITY CRAB CROQUETTES

Croquette Dough
3 small onions, finely
    chopped
4 cloves garlic, minced
½ cup finely chopped green
    pepper
1 teaspoon finely chopped
    hot red pepper
¼ cup plus 1 tablespoon
    vegetable oil
1 (6-ounce) can tomato paste
2 bay leaves
1¾ teaspoons salt, divided
½ teaspoon sugar
1 pound claw crabmeat,
    drained and flaked
6 eggs, beaten
1½ cups milk
¼ teaspoon pepper
3 cups cracker crumbs
1½ cups all-purpose flour
Additional vegetable oil

Ybor City Crab Croquettes have spicy filling, unusual coating.

Prepare Croquette Dough. Refrigerate 2 hours.

Sauté onion, garlic, green pepper, and red pepper in ¼ cup plus 1 tablespoon oil in a large heavy skillet 15 minutes. Stir in tomato paste, bay leaves, 1 teaspoon salt, and sugar. Cover and simmer 15 minutes over low heat. Add crabmeat; cover and simmer an additional 10 minutes. Remove from heat. Transfer mixture to a medium mixing bowl. Remove and discard bay leaves. Cover and refrigerate 2 hours.

Shape Croquette Dough into 36 two-inch balls. Press each ball into a 4-inch circle. Place 1 tablespoon chilled crabmeat mixture in center of each circle. Fold dough around crabmeat mixture to form boat-shaped croquette, sealing edges.

Combine eggs, milk, remaining salt, and pepper in a large mixing bowl; beat well.

Combine cracker crumbs and flour in a large mixing bowl; stir well. Dip each croquette in egg mixture; dredge in cracker crumb mixture. Repeat dipping and dredging procedure to heavily coat croquettes. Cover and refrigerate 2 hours.

Fry croquettes, a few at a time, in deep hot oil (375°) until golden brown. Drain well. Serve hot. Yield: 3 dozen.

Croquette Dough:

3 (1-pound) loaves white
    bread
1 (1-pound) loaf Cuban bread,
    sliced and toasted
1 tablespoon paprika
    (optional)
1 teaspoon salt

Trim crust from white bread; discard crust. Place bread in a large mixing bowl. Cover with water; let stand 15 minutes. Drain off water, and squeeze excess water from bread; return bread to large mixing bowl. Stir until doughy.

Place Cuban bread in container of an electric blender, a few slices at a time; process until breadcrumbs are fine. Repeat procedure with remaining toasted Cuban bread. Add breadcrumbs, paprika, if desired, and salt to white bread, mixing until soft dough forms. Cover and refrigerate dough until ready to use. Yield: dough for 3 dozen croquettes.

Note: 4¼ cups fine dry breadcrumbs may be substituted for 1-pound loaf of Cuban bread.

Cartons of fresh, refrigerated crabmeat are available in three forms: "Claw meat" is dark, but has a distinct nutty flavor; "regular" or "flake" is white meat, large and small, as it is picked; "lump" crab comes in large, unbroken pieces. Often tinged with red, flake is prime for salads and garnishes.

CRAB SAUCE LORENZO

2 large onions, chopped
1 green pepper, chopped
2 cloves garlic, minced
⅓ cup olive oil
3 cups tomato puree
3 cups water
1 (6-ounce) can tomato paste
1 bay leaf
2 tablespoons sugar
1 teaspoon salt
¼ teaspoon pepper
⅛ teaspoon dried whole
   oregano
⅛ teaspoon hot sauce
1 pound lump or flake
   crabmeat, drained
2 (8-ounce) packages thin
   spaghetti
Grated Parmesan cheese
Fresh parsley sprigs (optional)

Sauté onion, green pepper, and garlic in olive oil in a large Dutch oven until tender. Stir in next 9 ingredients, and bring to a boil. Reduce heat; simmer, uncovered, 2 hours, stirring frequently. Add crabmeat, stirring well. Simmer, uncovered, an additional 20 minutes, stirring frequently.

Cook spaghetti according to package directions. Remove bay leaf from crab sauce, and discard. Serve sauce over spaghetti, and top with cheese. Garnish with parsley, if desired. Yield: 6 servings.

CRABMEAT WITH CURRIED RICE

¾ cup butter or margarine
1 cup all-purpose flour
1 quart milk
1 teaspoon salt
¼ teaspoon pepper
2 tablespoons Worcestershire
   sauce
2 tablespoons sherry
2 pounds lump or flake
   crabmeat, drained
1 cup finely chopped celery
½ cup finely chopped green
   pepper
½ cup chopped pimiento
1½ cups (6 ounces) shredded
   sharp Cheddar cheese,
   divided
Paprika
Curried Rice

Melt butter in a medium saucepan; stir in flour, mixing well. Cook 1 minute, stirring constantly. Gradually add milk, stirring well. Cook over medium heat, stirring constantly, until thickened and bubbly. Remove sauce from heat. Stir in salt, pepper, Worcestershire sauce, and sherry.

Pour sauce into a large mixing bowl. Stir in crabmeat, celery, green pepper, pimiento, and 1 cup cheese; mix well. Lightly grease a 3-quart casserole; pour crabmeat mixture into dish. Top with remaining cheese; sprinkle with paprika. Bake at 350° for 1 hour.

Remove casserole from oven; serve immediately over Curried Rice. Yield: 10 to 12 servings.

Curried Rice:

2 (10½-ounce) cans chicken
   broth, undiluted
3 cups uncooked regular rice
1½ teaspoons curry powder
1 teaspoon salt

Bring chicken broth to a boil in a medium saucepan. Add rice and seasonings; reduce heat to low. Cover and simmer 20 minutes or until tender. Serve hot. Yield: 6 cups.

Nineteenth-century engraving of crabs on the seashore.

A seated banquet in a seafood restaurant, 1910. Decor was crab nets above and fish nets on the table.

SHE-CRAB SOUP

1 teaspoon butter or margarine
½ cup grated onion
½ teaspoon salt
Dash of pepper
1 tablespoon all-purpose flour
1 pound lump crabmeat
2 cups milk
½ cup whipping cream
½ teaspoon Worcestershire sauce
Sherry to taste

Melt butter in top of a double boiler over hot water. Add onion, salt, and pepper; stir well. Stir in flour, mixing well. Add crabmeat; cook 5 minutes.

Combine milk, whipping cream, and Worcestershire sauce. Gradually add milk mixture to crabmeat mixture, stirring well. Heat thoroughly. Ladle soup into individual serving bowls. Add sherry to taste. Serve immediately. Yield: about 1 quart.

CRAB LOUIS

½ cup mayonnaise
½ cup chili sauce
2 tablespoons chopped green pepper
2 tablespoons chopped sweet pickle
1 tablespoon finely chopped onion
1 tablespoon lemon juice
1 pound lump crabmeat
Leaf lettuce
2 medium tomatoes, peeled and quartered
2 small green peppers, seeded and cut into rings
2 hard-cooked eggs, sliced
Pimiento strips

Combine first 6 ingredients in a small mixing bowl; stir well. Add crabmeat, tossing lightly. Cover; chill thoroughly.

Spoon crabmeat mixture evenly onto 4 lettuce-lined plates. Garnish each plate with tomatoes, green pepper rings, egg slices, and pimiento strips. Yield: 4 servings.

BAYLEY'S ORIGINAL WEST INDIES SALAD

1 medium onion, finely chopped
1 pound lump crabmeat
½ teaspoon salt
½ teaspoon pepper
½ cup vegetable oil
¼ cup cider vinegar
½ cup cold water
Bibb lettuce leaves

Line the bottom of a large mixing bowl with half of chopped onion. Add crabmeat, and top with remaining chopped onion; sprinkle with salt and pepper.

Pour oil, vinegar, and water, in order, over crabmeat mixture. (Do not stir.) Cover and chill 2 to 12 hours.

Toss lightly, and serve on individual lettuce-lined serving plates. Yield: 4 servings.

CRAYFISH

BOILED CRAYFISH

5 medium onions, halved
5 lemons, halved
6 cloves garlic, halved
4 bay leaves
1¼ pounds salt
Red pepper to taste
10 pounds whole crayfish

Place onions, lemons, garlic, and bay leaves in a cheesecloth bag. Place bag in a small amount of water in a large stockpot. Stir in salt and pepper. Place over medium heat, and cook 30 minutes.

Add additional water to accommodate crayfish. Bring to a boil; add crayfish, maintaining boiling point of water. Boil, uncovered, 7 minutes. Remove cheesecloth bag; discard. Drain crayfish; peel and eat immediately. Yield: 20 to 25 servings.

FRIED CRAYFISH

1 pound crayfish tails, peeled
1½ teaspoons salt, divided
½ teaspoon pepper, divided
½ cup milk
2 eggs, lightly beaten
2½ cups all-purpose flour
Vegetable oil
Cocktail sauce (page 126)

Sprinkle crayfish tails with ½ teaspoon salt and ¼ teaspoon pepper; set aside.

Combine milk, eggs, and ½ teaspoon salt in a medium mixing bowl; mix well. Add crayfish, and stir until moistened.

Combine flour, remaining salt, and pepper in a large mixing bowl; mix well. Add half of crayfish tails, tossing gently until well coated. Repeat procedure with remaining crayfish.

Heat ½ inch oil in a 9-inch skillet to 350°. Fry crayfish tails, a few at a time, until lightly browned; drain on paper towels. Serve immediately with cocktail sauce. Yield: 4 servings.

CRAYFISH JAMBALAYA

12 large green peppers
1 cup chopped onion
½ cup chopped celery
4 cloves garlic, minced
½ cup butter or margarine
2 (14½-ounce) cans whole tomatoes, chopped
2 tablespoons chopped fresh parsley
1 tablespoon salt
¾ teaspoon pepper
½ teaspoon red pepper
1 pound crayfish tails, peeled
1 cup chopped onion
4 cups hot cooked rice

Cut off tops of green peppers; chop ½ cup, and set aside. Remove and discard seeds from bottoms. Parboil bottoms, and set aside.

Sauté chopped pepper, onion, celery, and garlic in butter in a large iron pot until tender. Add tomatoes, parsley, salt, and pepper; stir well. Cook, uncovered, 40 minutes over low heat. Add crayfish tails; cook 10 minutes. Stir in onion and rice. Cover; steam 5 minutes.

Spoon jambalaya into prepared green peppers. Place on individual serving plates; serve warm. Yield: 12 servings.

In Louisiana, crayfish are called crawfish. Here they race at the Breaux Bridge Crawfish Festival.

Photographer: Turner Browne

Crayfish Pie (front), Crayfish Étouffée in Dutch oven, and Jambalaya in peppers.

CRAYFISH PIE

3 cups all-purpose flour
1¼ teaspoons salt, divided
1 cup plus 2 tablespoons shortening
6 to 9 tablespoons cold water
1 cup chopped onion
1 cup chopped celery
2 cloves garlic, minced
½ cup butter or margarine
1 tablespoon cornstarch
¼ cup chicken broth
1 cup whipping cream
1 pound crayfish tails, peeled and cooked
¼ teaspoon white pepper
⅛ teaspoon red pepper

Combine flour and ¾ teaspoon salt in a medium bowl; cut in shortening with a pastry blender until mixture resembles coarse meal. Sprinkle water over surface of flour mixture; stir with a fork until dry ingredients are moistened. Shape dough into a ball; chill.

Sauté onion, celery, and garlic in butter in a large skillet until tender. Combine cornstarch and chicken broth; stir until well blended. Add chicken broth mixture and whipping cream to sautéed vegetables, mixing well. Stir in crayfish tails, remaining salt, and pepper; set aside.

Roll half of pastry to ⅛-inch thickness on a lightly floured surface; fit into a 9-inch pie-plate. Spoon crayfish filling into pastry shell.

Roll remaining pastry to ⅛-inch thickness; cut into ¾-inch-wide strips, and arrange in a lattice fashion over filling. Trim bottom pastry, and arrange lattice pastry in a decorative design on edges.

Bake at 350° for 45 minutes or until crust is golden brown. Yield: one 9-inch pie.

CRAYFISH ÉTOUFFÉE

4 large onions, chopped
4 medium-size green peppers, chopped
4 cloves garlic, minced
2 stalks celery, chopped
1 cup butter or margarine
2 tablespoons all-purpose flour
4 pounds crayfish tails, peeled
2 cups hot water
2 teaspoons salt
¼ teaspoon pepper
¼ teaspoon red pepper
¼ cup chopped green onion tops
¼ cup chopped fresh parsley
Hot cooked rice

Sauté onion, green pepper, garlic, and celery in butter in a large Dutch oven over low heat 30 minutes. Stir in flour. Add crayfish tails, water, salt, and pepper. Cover and simmer 10 minutes or until crayfish are tender. Stir in onion and parsley. Serve over hot cooked rice. Yield: 8 to 10 servings.

CRAYFISH BISQUE

8 pounds whole crayfish, cooked
¼ cup bacon drippings
¼ cup butter or margarine
½ cup all-purpose flour
2 cups finely chopped onion
1 cup finely chopped celery
½ cup finely chopped green pepper
1 clove garlic, minced
4 cups hot water
2 (15-ounce) cans tomato sauce with tomato bits
¼ cup chopped fresh parsley
2 tablespoons lemon juice
2 bay leaves
1 teaspoon dried thyme leaves, crushed
1 teaspoon salt
½ teaspoon red pepper
8 whole allspice
3 cups hot cooked rice
48 Stuffed Crayfish Heads

Break off crayfish tails, snap in half lengthwise, and lift out meat in one piece; discard tail shells. Snap off large claws (if desired, break claws with nut-cracker, and remove bits of meat) and smaller legs; discard. Cut off top of head just behind eyes; discard. Scoop body shell clean, carefully removing and reserving yellow fat; discard intestinal matter. Clean and thoroughly wash 48 body shells, referred to as crayfish heads; set aside. Grind tail meat to yield 3 cups, reserving 1 cup for bisque and remaining 2 cups for Stuffed Crayfish Heads.

Melt bacon drippings and butter in a large Dutch oven over medium-low heat; add flour and cook, stirring constantly, 15 minutes or until browned. Add onion, celery, green pepper, and garlic, mixing well. Cover and cook 5 minutes or until tender. Gradually stir in water. Add tomato sauce, parsley, lemon juice, bay leaves, thyme, salt, pepper, and allspice; mix well. Stir in 1 cup crayfish meat and reserved crayfish fat. Cover and bring to a boil. Reduce heat; cover and simmer 1 hour, stirring occasionally. Remove bay leaves and whole allspice.

To serve, ladle into individual soup bowls over hot cooked rice, and place 6 Stuffed Crayfish Heads in each bowl. Yield: 8 servings.

Stuffed Crayfish Heads:

½ cup butter or margarine
1 cup finely chopped onion
½ cup finely chopped celery
1 clove garlic, minced
¼ cup chopped fresh parsley
1 teaspoon salt
¼ teaspoon red pepper
2 cups reserved crayfish meat
2 cups soft breadcrumbs
48 empty crayfish head shells
½ cup all-purpose flour
Vegetable oil

Melt butter in a large skillet. Add onion, celery, and garlic. Cover and cook 5 minutes or until tender. Stir in parsley, salt, pepper, and crayfish meat. Add breadcrumbs, mixing well. Stuff mixture into empty heads.

Roll heads in flour. Place in a single layer in fryer basket. Fry in deep hot oil (350°) for 3 minutes or until lightly brown; drain. Keep warm until ready to serve. Yield: 4 dozen.

Parade of crayfish costumes, No-Tsu-Oh (Houston, spelled backwards) festival, 1914.

LOBSTER

ARNAUD'S LOBSTER THERMIDOR

8 quarts water
½ cup salt
4 (1¾-pound) live lobsters
1 cup plus 3 tablespoons
   butter or margarine,
   divided
1 cup all-purpose flour
2 cups milk
3 egg yolks, lightly beaten
½ pound fresh mushrooms,
   chopped
¼ cup chopped green
   onion
Grated Parmesan cheese

Combine water and salt in a large stockpot; bring to a boil. Grasp each lobster just behind the eyes, and plunge headfirst into boiling water. Return to a boil; cover and boil 5 minutes for first pound, 3 more minutes for each additional pound. Remove lobsters from water with kitchen tongs; plunge into cold water. Drain.

Lay cooked lobster, back side up, on a wooden cutting board. Tuck the tail underneath the body; insert the tip of a large sharp knife into the joint where the head and tail portions come together. Split the tail sections into two halves.

Turn the lobster around, and cut through the head portion, dividing the lobster into two separate pieces. Remove and discard the greenish-gray stomach pouch and the sand sac from the head.

Remove the tail meat and all the white meat from the body of the lobster. Crack the claws, and remove all meat. Coarsely chop the lobster meat, and set aside. Break away and discard the body portion of the shell. Rinse and thoroughly drain the tail section of the shell, and set tail aside.

Melt 1 cup butter in a large heavy saucepan over low heat; add flour, stirring until smooth. Cook 1 minute, stirring constantly. Gradually add milk; cook over medium heat, stirring constantly, until thickened and bubbly. Remove from heat; gradually stir one-fourth of hot mixture into yolks. Add to remaining hot mixture, stirring constantly. Return to medium heat; cook, stirring constantly, until sauce is smooth and thickened. Set aside.

Sauté mushrooms and onion in remaining butter in a large skillet. Add lobster meat, and cook over medium heat, stirring frequently, until thoroughly heated. Gently fold lobster mixture into sauce.

Place lobster shells in a 2½-quart shallow baking dish; spoon lobster mixture into and around shells. Sprinkle generously with cheese; broil 6 inches from heating element 1 minute or until cheese is lightly browned. Serve immediately. Yield: 4 servings.

Arnaud's Lobster Thermidor is a favorite among the treats which have contributed to the culinary fame of New Orleans.

HOW TO REMOVE MEAT FROM A LOBSTER

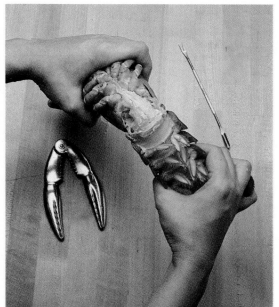

Step 1 — Grasp the lobster in both hands, turning so that the soft side faces up. Bend the lobster until the tailpiece separates from the body. Remove the tail flippers by bending back until they crack off from base of tail.

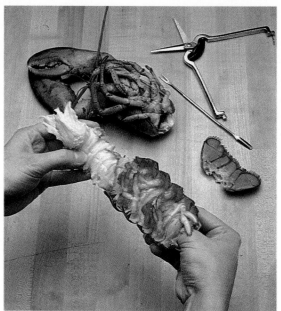

Step 2 — Insert thumb at the point where the tail flippers were removed. Gently push the meat out through the open end as far as possible; grasp meat with other hand, and pull out.

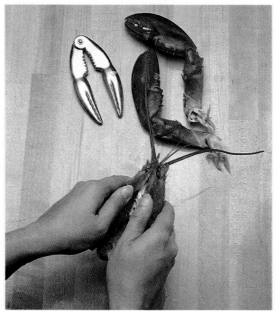

Step 3 — Break off the large claws and legs where they are attached to the chest; set aside. Grasp the chest portion of the lobster in both hands, and crack or cut the shell apart. The greenish tomalley or liver and coral, if any, may be eaten.

Step 4 — Using lobster crackers or a mallet, crack the shell of the large claws. Gently pull the shell apart to remove the claw meat. A lobster fork may be used to remove additional meat from the claws and legs of the lobster.

HOW TO STEAM LOBSTER

Water
3 tablespoons vinegar
1 teaspoon dry mustard
2 (1- to 1¼-pound) live
   lobsters
Clarified butter (page 127)

Place a steamer rack in a large stockpot and add water to a depth of ½ inch below rack. Add vinegar and mustard; bring to a boil. Grasp each lobster just behind the eyes and place on rack. Cover with a tight fitting lid. Steam over high heat 12 minutes. (Do not remove lid during steaming procedure.) Lobster will be bright red when done. Remove lobsters from stockpot with kitchen tongs. Reserve stock for use in other recipes.

Serve whole lobsters immediately with clarified butter or remove meat for use in other recipes. (See how-to procedure for removing meat from shell). Yield: 2 servings.

HOW TO BOIL LOBSTER

4 quarts water
¼ cup salt
2 (1- to 1¼-pound) live
   lobsters
Clarified butter (page 127)

Combine water and salt in a large stockpot; bring to a boil. Grasp each lobster just behind the eyes, and quickly rinse under cold water. Plunge lobsters headfirst into boiling water. Return water to a boil; cover and boil 5 minutes for first pound, 3 more minutes for each additional pound. Remove lobsters from water.

Serve lobsters immediately with clarified butter. (See how-to procedure for removing meat from shell.) Yield: 2 servings.

Note: If lobster meat is to be used for other recipes, plunge lobster into cold water. Drain. Remove meat and use as directed in recipe. Yield: 3 cups lobster meat.

BOILED LOBSTER WITH DILL SAUCE

8 quarts water
½ cup salt
4 (1¾-pound) live lobsters
Fresh dill sprigs
Dill Sauce

Combine water and salt in a large stockpot; bring to a boil. Grasp each lobster just behind the eyes, and plunge headfirst into boiling water. Return to a boil; cover and boil 5 minutes for first pound, 3 more minutes for each additional pound. Remove lobsters from water with kitchen tongs; plunge into cold water. Drain.

Position lobster on its back on a cutting board. With a sharp knife or kitchen shears, cut entire length of lobster from head to tail. Cut down outside edges of tail to remove membranous covering and expose meat. Loosen meat at end of tail, and remove gently with a fork. Remove meat from claws. Cover lobster meat and chill.

Arrange lobster meat on a serving platter; garnish with dill sprigs. Serve with Dill Sauce. Yield: 4 servings.

Dill Sauce:

⅓ cup olive oil
Juice of 1 lemon
2 tablespoons grated onion
   (optional)
1 tablespoon finely chopped
   fresh dill
1 teaspoon salt
½ teaspoon dry mustard
¼ teaspoon pepper

Combine all ingredients in a small mixing bowl; mix well. Chill. Yield: ½ cup.

LOBSTER THERMIDOR

2 quarts water
4 frozen lobster tails,
   thawed
¼ cup butter or margarine
¼ cup all-purpose flour
1½ cups whipping cream
1 egg yolk, beaten
1 cup sliced fresh
   mushrooms
1 tablespoon chopped
   fresh chives
½ teaspoon salt
½ teaspoon dry mustard
2 tablespoons sherry
½ cup grated Parmesan
   cheese, divided
Paprika

Bring water to a boil in a large Dutch oven; add lobster tails. Return to a boil; cook 5 minutes. Remove tails from water with kitchen tongs; rinse under cold water. Drain.

Split lobster tails lengthwise, leaving bottoms of shells attached. Remove meat, and cut into bite-size pieces. Set meat aside. Rinse shells thoroughly, and let dry. Press shells open flat, and place in a 13- x 9- x 2-inch baking dish.

Melt butter in a heavy saucepan over low heat; add flour, stirring until smooth. Cook 1 minute, stirring constantly. Gradually add whipping cream; cook over medium heat, stirring constantly, until thickened.

Gradually stir 2 tablespoons hot mixture into yolk; add to remaining hot mixture, stirring constantly. Stir in mushrooms, chives, salt, and mustard. Cook over low heat 2 to 3 minutes. Remove from heat; stir in sherry and reserved lobster.

Sprinkle 1 teaspoon cheese in each lobster shell. Spoon lobster mixture evenly into shells. Sprinkle with remaining cheese and paprika. Bake at 375° for 15 minutes or until browned. Serve immediately. Yield: 4 servings.

GRILLED LOBSTER TAILS

¼ cup plus 2 tablespoons butter, melted
2 tablespoons lemon juice
½ teaspoon salt
⅛ teaspoon pepper
⅛ teaspoon tarragon
6 frozen lobster tails, thawed

Combine first 5 ingredients, stir well. Set aside.

Split lobster tails lengthwise, cutting through upper shell and meat to, but not through, bottom shell. Press shell halves apart to expose meat. Place lobster tails, shell side down, on grill. Baste with sauce, and cook over medium coals 20 minutes. Turn, and cook 5 minutes. Remove from grill; serve with sauce. Yield: 6 servings.

BROILED LOBSTER TAILS

4 frozen lobster tails, thawed
½ teaspoon salt
¼ teaspoon pepper
2 tablespoons lime juice, divided
1 tablespoon Worcestershire sauce
3 tablespoons butter or margarine, divided
2 tablespoons grated Parmesan cheese
¾ cup water
2 slices bacon, halved

Split lobster tails lengthwise; cut through upper shell and meat to, but not through, bottom shell. Press shell halves open. Place in a 13- x 9- x 2-inch baking pan; sprinkle with salt, pepper, 1 tablespoon lime juice, and Worcestershire sauce. Dot with 2 tablespoons butter; sprinkle with cheese.

Pour water in bottom of pan; add remaining lime juice and butter to water. Broil 4 inches from heating element 4 minutes. Top with bacon, and broil an additional 3 minutes.

Remove lobster tails to a serving platter. Pour sauce in pan over broiled lobster, and serve. Yield: 4 servings.

Collection of M.E. Warren

Eriosson Pier, Betterton, Md.

Postcard from Eriosson Pier, Betterton, Maryland, c.1900.

LOBSTER TAILS WITH CUCUMBER SAUCE

2 quarts water
2 tablespoons vinegar
1 teaspoon salt
1 teaspoon dry mustard
½ teaspoon pepper
2 bay leaves
4 (½-pound) frozen lobster tails, thawed
Cucumber Sauce
Cucumber slices (optional)

Combine water, vinegar, salt, mustard, pepper, and bay leaves in a large Dutch oven; bring to a boil. Add lobster tails; return to a boil, and cook 5 minutes. Remove lobster tails from water with kitchen tongs. Rinse under cold water. Drain.

With a sharp knife or kitchen shears, cut down outer edges of tails to remove membranous covering and expose meat. Remove the entire tail section of meat, and cut into ½-inch-thick slices. Return meat to shell; cover and chill.

Place lobster tails on individual serving dishes; top with Cucumber Sauce. Garnish with cucumber slices, if desired. Yield: 4 servings.

Cucumber Sauce:

1 cup grated cucumber, drained and patted dry
1 small onion, chopped
½ cup commercial sour cream
1 tablespoon vinegar
¼ teaspoon salt
Pinch of sugar
Dash of red pepper
1 drop green food coloring

Combine all ingredients in a small mixing bowl; stir well. Cover and chill at least 1 hour. Yield: 1½ cups.

The rock or spiny lobster is plentiful off the Florida coast and in the entire Gulf and Caribbean area. But demand so far exceeds supply that we must import quantities, frozen, from South Africa, Australia, New Zealand, and Chile. Rock lobster is the name under which the spiny is merchandised: two names for the same creature. By any name, it is not a lobster, but a salt water relative of the crayfish. It has no claws; only the tail is eaten. Rock lobster is the *langouste* of French culinary fame.

For Grilled Lobster Tails, we use rock lobster.

LOBSTER IN SHERRY SAUCE

6 cups water
8 frozen lobster tails, thawed
½ cup butter
1 medium onion, grated and
  juice reserved
2 teaspoons dry mustard
1 teaspoon salt
¼ cup plus 2 tablespoons
  all-purpose flour
2 cups milk
Dash of hot sauce
2 tablespoons lemon juice
3 to 4 tablespoons sherry
2 tablespoons grated
  Parmesan cheese
8 baked commercial patty
  shells

Bring water to a boil in a large Dutch oven; add lobster tails, and return to a boil. Cook 5 minutes. Remove tails from water with kitchen tongs, and rinse under cold water. Drain.

Position tails on their backs on a cutting board. With a sharp knife or kitchen shears, cut down the outer edges of tails to remove membranous covering and expose meat. Remove meat, and cut into bite-size pieces. Set meat aside.

Melt butter in a heavy saucepan over low heat; add onion and juice, cooking until tender.

Add mustard and salt, mixing well. Add flour, stirring until smooth. Cook 1 minute, stirring constantly. Gradually add milk; cook over medium heat, stirring constantly, until mixture is thickened and bubbly. Stir in hot sauce, lemon juice, sherry, Parmesan cheese, and reserved lobster. Continue cooking until lobster is thoroughly heated. Spoon lobster mixture into patty shells, and serve immediately. Yield: 8 servings.

Steaming lobsters for packing was a hazardous job. Frank Leslie's Illustrated Weekly, *1877.*

Shellfish Series Collection, Georgetown, Delaware

A display of manly courage is pictured on this trade card, c.1900.

CREAMED LOBSTER

½ cup butter or margarine
½ cup all-purpose flour
2 cups whipping cream
2 cups chopped, cooked lobster
1 medium-size green pepper, chopped
1 whole pimiento, chopped
½ teaspoon salt
½ teaspoon white pepper
Toast Baskets
Fresh parsley sprigs

Melt butter in a large heavy saucepan over low heat; add flour, stirring until smooth. Cook 1 minute, stirring constantly. Gradually add whipping cream; cook over medium heat, stirring constantly, until thickened and bubbly. Remove from heat. Fold in lobster, green pepper, pimiento, salt, and pepper.

Spoon ¼ cup mixture into each basket. Garnish with parsley, and serve. Yield: 8 servings.

Toast Baskets:

16 slices bread
Softened butter or margarine

Trim crust from bread slices; lightly butter both sides. Press each slice into an 8-ounce custard cup. Bake at 350° for 15 minutes or until lightly browned. Remove baskets from custard cups; cool completely on wire racks. Yield: 16 baskets.

CURRIED LOBSTER

2 quarts water
4 frozen lobster tails, thawed
1 medium onion, chopped
1 cooking apple, peeled, cored, and chopped
¼ cup butter
3 tablespoons all-purpose flour
½ teaspoon salt
1 cup chicken broth
1 cup warm whipping cream
1 teaspoon curry powder
Hot cooked rice
Condiments

Bring water to a boil in a large Dutch oven. Add lobster tails; return to a boil and cook 5 minutes. Remove tails from water with kitchen tongs; rinse under cold water. Drain.

With a sharp knife, cut down outer edge of tail to remove shell. Remove meat; cut into chunks. Discard shell.

Sauté onion and apple in butter in a small skillet; stir in flour and salt. Add chicken broth; cook over low heat, stirring constantly, until sauce begins to thicken. Stir in whipping cream; cook until sauce is smooth and thickened. Add curry powder; stir well. Add reserved lobster; cook until lobster is thoroughly heated.

Spoon over rice, and serve with several of the following: (about 1 cup each) chutney, flaked coconut, chopped hard-cooked egg, crumbled bacon, salted peanuts, and raisins. Yield: 6 servings.

LOBSTER NEWBURG

1 teaspoon finely chopped green pepper
¼ cup butter
2 cups coarsely chopped, cooked lobster
2 tablespoons sherry
2 tablespoons cognac
½ cup whipping cream
3 egg yolks, well beaten
½ teaspoon ground nutmeg
⅛ teaspoon red pepper
Salt to taste
6 baked commercial patty shells

Sauté green pepper in butter in a large skillet 3 minutes. Stir in lobster, sherry, and cognac; cook 1 minute over medium heat. Add whipping cream; remove from heat. Gradually stir in yolks, nutmeg, pepper, and salt. Cook over low heat 2 minutes or until mixture is slightly thickened. Spoon evenly into patty shells. Serve immediately. Yield: 6 servings.

LOBSTER COCKTAIL

½ cup catsup
¼ cup lemon juice
2 teaspoons Worcestershire sauce
½ teaspoon chopped chives
½ teaspoon hot sauce
⅛ teaspoon salt
1 cup coarsely chopped, cooked lobster
Lettuce leaves

Combine first 6 ingredients in a medium mixing bowl; mix well. Stir in lobster; cover and chill at least 1 hour.

Spoon mixture into lettuce-lined cocktail glasses; serve. Yield: 4 appetizer servings.

OYSTERS

OYSTERS WITH COCKTAIL SAUCE

1 cup catsup
2 tablespoons lemon juice
1 tablespoon finely chopped onion
12 drops hot sauce
1 teaspoon horseradish
2 large lemons, halved
2 dozen oysters on the half shell

Combine first 5 ingredients; mix well, and chill.

Cut a thin slice from the bottom of each lemon half so that it sits flat. Gently remove membrane, leaving lemon shell intact. Fill each lemon shell with prepared cocktail sauce, and place shells in center of a deep dish filled with crushed ice. Arrange six oysters around each bowl of sauce, and serve immediately. Yield: 4 servings.

STEAMED OYSTERS

2 dozen unshucked oysters
1 tablespoon salt
Melted butter
Cocktail sauce

Scrub and rinse oysters thoroughly in cold water; drain.

Pour water into a large stockpot with a steaming basket to come 2 inches below basket. Add salt; bring to a boil.

Place oysters in basket; cover and steam 10 minutes or until shells open. Drain.

Using an oyster knife, remove top shell and loosen oyster meat. Place oysters on the half shell on a large serving platter. Serve with melted butter or cocktail sauce. Yield: 2 dozen.

BROILED OYSTERS

1 dozen unshucked oysters
¼ teaspoon Worcestershire sauce
⅛ teaspoon hot sauce
3 slices bacon, cut into pieces
Dash of paprika

Rinse oysters thoroughly in cold water. Shuck oysters, reserving deep half of shells. Arrange oysters in a single layer in a shallow baking pan.

Combine sauces; brush oysters with sauce mixture. Place a piece of bacon on each oyster; sprinkle with paprika.

Broil 4 inches from heating element 3 to 4 minutes; serve immediately. Yield: 1 dozen.

SAUTÉED OYSTERS ON TOAST

2 (12-ounce) containers Select oysters, undrained
6 slices bacon
¼ cup butter or margarine
Toast points
Fresh parsley sprigs

Drain oysters on paper towels; set aside. Cook bacon in a large heavy skillet until crisp; drain well on paper towels, and set aside. Drain bacon drippings,

and reserve for other uses.

Sauté oysters in butter in skillet until edges of oysters begin to curl.

Arrange toast points on a serving platter; top with oysters, and spoon remaining butter from skillet over oysters. Garnish with reserved bacon and parsley. Serve immediately. Yield: 4 servings.

MARYLAND PAN-FRIED OYSTERS

2 eggs, beaten
2 tablespoons milk
1 teaspoon salt
Dash of pepper
1½ cups fine, dry breadcrumbs
1½ cups all-purpose flour
2 (12-ounce) containers Select oysters, drained
Vegetable oil
Cocktail sauce (optional)

Combine eggs, milk, salt, and pepper in a small mixing bowl. Combine breadcrumbs and flour in a medium mixing bowl. Dredge oysters in breadcrumb mixture; dip in egg mixture, and roll in breadcrumb mixture.

Fry in ½ inch hot oil for 3 minutes on each side or until golden brown. Drain well on paper towels. Serve immediately with cocktail sauce, if desired. Yield: 4 to 6 servings.

An oyster roast at the Paca House, Annapolis: (clockwise from front) Broiled Oysters, Maryland Pan-Fried Oysters, Oysters with Cocktail Sauce, and Steamed Oysters.

SOUTHERN FRIED OYSTERS

¾ cup yellow cornmeal
⅓ cup all-purpose flour
½ teaspoon salt
2 (12-ounce) containers
  Select oysters, drained
Vegetable oil
Fresh parsley sprigs
Lemon wedges

Combine cornmeal, flour, and salt. Dredge oysters in cornmeal mixture.

Fry oysters in deep hot oil (375°) until oysters float to the top and are golden brown; drain well on paper towels. Transfer oysters to a serving platter; garnish with parsley and lemon wedges. Yield: 2 dozen.

CREAMED OYSTERS

2 cups water
2 (12-ounce) containers
  Standard oysters, drained
½ cup butter or margarine
½ cup all-purpose flour
1 teaspoon salt
¼ teaspoon pepper
⅛ teaspoon mace
2 bay leaves
1½ cups milk
3 tablespoons sherry
8 slices toast

Bring water to a boil in a large heavy saucepan. Place oysters in boiling water; remove from heat, and let stand 5 minutes. Place oysters in a colander to drain, reserving 1 cup water. Set oysters and water aside.

Melt butter in a large saucepan over low heat; add flour, stirring until smooth. Cook 1 minute, stirring constantly. Stir in salt, pepper, mace, and bay leaves. Gradually add milk and reserved 1 cup water; cook over medium heat, stirring constantly, until mixture is thickened and bubbly. Add drained oysters, and cook 2 minutes. Remove from heat; stir in sherry. Remove and discard bay leaves. Serve immediately over toast. Yield: 8 servings.

HOW TO SHUCK AN OYSTER

Step 1 — Clean and scrub oyster shell with a stiff brush under cold running water. With gloved hand and an oyster knife, grip the oyster tightly in one hand, and force the oyster knife into the side opposite the hinge.

Step 2 — With a twist of the knife blade, slowly force the oyster shell open. Slice through the large muscle attached to the flat upper shell. Remove upper shell.

Step 3 — Cut the lower end of the same muscle which is attached to the deep half of the shell to loosen the oyster from the shell. Remove any shell chips that cling to the meat.

Men work at tonging oysters in Louisiana, c.1915.

ANGELS ON HORSEBACK

2 (12-ounce) containers
　Select oysters, drained
12 slices bacon, halved
½ cup milk
1 egg, beaten
1 cup all-purpose flour
¼ teaspoon baking powder
⅛ teaspoon salt
Vegetable oil

Wrap each oyster with half a slice of bacon; secure with a wooden pick.

Combine milk and egg; beat well. Combine flour, baking powder, and salt; stir well. Dip prepared oysters in egg mixture; dredge in flour mixture. Repeat dipping and dredging procedure with each oyster-bacon roll.

Fry in deep hot oil (375°) until oysters float to the top and are golden brown. Drain on paper towels. Serve immediately. Yield: 8 appetizer servings.

SMOKEHOUSE OYSTERS

2 cups hickory chips, soaked
　in water
Rock salt
1 dozen oysters on the half
　shell, drained
⅛ teaspoon salt
⅛ teaspoon pepper
¼ cup butter or margarine,
　softened
2 tablespoons finely chopped
　green onion
2 tablespoons finely chopped
　fresh parsley
3 tablespoons cornflake
　crumbs
3 tablespoons grated
　Parmesan cheese
Fresh parsley sprigs

Prepare charcoal fire in grill, and let burn 10 to 15 minutes. Sprinkle wet hickory chips over gray-white coals. Cover grill with lid.

Sprinkle a thin layer of rock salt in an aluminum foil-lined 13- x 9- x 2-inch pan. Arrange oysters (in shells) over rock salt; sprinkle oysters with ⅛ teaspoon salt and pepper.

Combine butter, green onion, and chopped parsley; dot each oyster with butter mixture. Combine cornflake crumbs and cheese, and sprinkle over butter mixture.

Place pan on grill 4 inches from hot coals and wet hickory chips. Cover grill with lid. Grill 20 minutes or until crumbs are browned and oyster edges curl. Garnish with parsley sprigs. Yield: 4 appetizer servings.

Note: Rock salt is used to hold shells upright and to keep oysters hot.

Louisville's Oyster Inn, decorated with oyster shells, sold fried oysters for 5¢ in 1930.

LOUISVILLE ROLLED OYSTERS

½ cup all-purpose flour
1 teaspoon baking powder
½ teaspoon salt
½ cup milk
1 egg, beaten
1 cup cornmeal
1½ dozen shucked oysters, drained
Vegetable oil
Catsup or tartar sauce (page 126)

Combine flour, baking powder, and salt in a large mixing bowl; mix well. Combine milk and egg; add to flour mixture, stirring well. Place cornmeal in a large mixing bowl.

Place oysters in flour mixture. Remove three oysters at a time, forming a ball. Roll in cornmeal. Place in flour mixture to coat; roll again in cornmeal. Repeat double coating procedure with remaining oysters, making 6 oyster rolls.

Place rolls in fryer basket. Deep fry in hot oil (375°). Reduce temperature to 350° and cook until rolls float to the top and are golden brown; drain well on paper towels. Serve with catsup or tartar sauce. Yield: 6 servings.

The rolled oyster, which is actually a handful of oysters clad in an overcoat of crumbs, is a Louisville, Kentucky, phenomenon. Kolb's and Mazzoni's were famous for them in the '30s, and Mazzoni's still is, having survived the move from its original aromatic deep-fried location into a shiny new office building in the downtown business district of Louisville.

SCALLOPED OYSTERS

½ cup butter or margarine, melted
2 cups coarsely crumbled cracker crumbs
2 (12-ounce) containers Select oysters, undrained
½ teaspoon pepper, divided
About ½ cup half-and-half
½ teaspoon salt
¼ teaspoon Worcestershire sauce
Dash of hot sauce

Pour melted butter over cracker crumbs in a medium mixing bowl; toss gently until well combined. Drain oysters, reserving liquor. Place one-third of cracker crumb mixture in a buttered 8-inch round cakepan; top with half of oysters, and sprinkle with half of pepper. Repeat procedure.

Add enough half-and-half to oyster liquor to equal 1 cup. Add salt, Worcestershire sauce, and hot sauce; stir well. Pour over oysters; top with remaining cracker crumb mixture. Bake at 350° for 40 minutes. Serve hot. Yield: 4 servings.

OYSTERS CASINO

3 slices bacon, diced
¼ cup chopped onion
2 tablespoons chopped green pepper
2 tablespoons chopped celery
1 teaspoon lemon juice
½ teaspoon salt
⅛ teaspoon pepper
½ teaspoon Worcestershire sauce
2 drops hot sauce
1 (12-ounce) container Select oysters, drained

Cook bacon in a skillet until crisp. Add onion, green pepper, and celery; cook until tender. Add remaining ingredients, except oysters; stir well.

Place oysters in a well-greased 10- x 6- x 2-inch baking dish. Spread bacon mixture over oysters. Bake at 350° for 20 minutes or until oyster edges curl. Yield: 4 servings.

OYSTERS BIENVILLE

2 (12-ounce) containers Standard oysters, undrained
2 tablespoons butter or margarine
2 tablespoons all-purpose flour
2 cups chopped green onion
1 (4-ounce) can sliced mushrooms, drained and chopped
1 tablespoon minced fresh parsley
½ cup Chablis or other dry white wine
2 egg yolks
½ pound medium shrimp, cooked, peeled, deveined, and chopped
½ teaspoon salt
¼ teaspoon pepper
¼ cup plus 2 tablespoons soft breadcrumbs
¼ cup grated Parmesan cheese

Drain oysters, reserving ¾ cup liquor; set aside.

Melt butter in a large heavy skillet; add flour, stirring to blend. Sauté green onion in butter mixture until tender. Stir in mushrooms, parsley, wine, and reserved oyster liquor; simmer over medium heat until thoroughly heated.

Beat yolks. Add a small amount of hot mixture to yolks; add to remaining hot mixture, stirring well. Cook over low heat, stirring frequently, until mixture thickens. Remove from heat, and stir in shrimp, salt, and pepper. Set aside.

Arrange oysters in 12 individual baking shells or ramekins. Spoon ¼ cup shrimp mixture into each. Combine breadcrumbs and cheese; sprinkle evenly over mixture in shells. Bake at 350° for 15 minutes or until lightly browned on top. Serve immediately. Yield: 12 servings.

OYSTERS ROCKEFELLER

2 dozen unshucked oysters
¾ cup soft breadcrumbs
¼ cup butter or margarine, melted
3 tablespoons sherry
1 cup finely chopped fresh spinach
¼ cup finely chopped onion
1 teaspoon seasoned salt
1 teaspoon Worcestershire sauce
Rock salt
¼ cup grated Parmesan cheese
Lemon wedges
Fresh parsley sprigs

Rinse oysters in cold water. Shuck oysters, reserving deep half of shells; place oysters in colander to drain. Set aside.

Combine breadcrumbs, butter, and sherry; set aside. Combine spinach, onion, seasoned salt, and Worcestershire sauce, and set aside.

Sprinkle a layer of rock salt in bottom of a large broiling pan. Place oysters in half shells; arrange shells on rock salt. Top oysters evenly with spinach mixture. Sprinkle with cheese; top evenly with breadcrumb mixture. Bake at 400° for 15 minutes. Broil 4 inches from heating element 2 minutes or until browned. Garnish with lemon wedges and parsley sprigs. Yield: 4 servings.

Currier and Ives lithograph, Nice and Tempting, *from the 1800s.*

OYSTER SOUFFLÉ

3 tablespoons butter or
   margarine
¼ cup all-purpose flour
½ teaspoon salt
Dash of paprika
1 cup milk
4 eggs, separated
1½ cups oysters, drained and
   minced (about 1 cup)

Melt butter in a large heavy saucepan over low heat; add flour and seasonings, stirring until smooth. Cook 1 minute, stirring constantly. Gradually add milk; cook over medium heat, stirring constantly, until thickened and bubbly.

Beat egg yolks until thick and lemon colored. Gradually stir one-fourth of hot white sauce into yolks; add to remaining hot white sauce.

Beat egg whites (at room temperature) until stiff but not dry. Gently fold egg whites and minced oysters into hot white sauce. Spoon mixture into a lightly greased 1½-quart soufflé dish. Place dish in a 13- x 9- x 2-inch baking pan; pour hot water into pan to a depth of 1 inch. Bake at 350° for 45 minutes or until puffed. Serve immediately. Yield: 6 servings.

OYSTER PO-BOYS

2 (12-ounce) containers
   Standard oysters, drained
½ teaspoon salt
¼ teaspoon pepper
⅛ teaspoon red pepper
¾ cup yellow cornmeal
Peanut oil
1 (16-ounce) loaf French
   bread
¼ cup mayonnaise
¼ cup catsup
Lettuce leaves
Tomato slices
Dill pickle slices

Season oysters with salt and pepper; dredge in cornmeal.

Heat 1 inch of oil to 350°. Add oysters and cook until golden brown; drain on paper towels.

Cut French bread into 4 sections; slice each section open. Spread mayonnaise on one side and catsup on the other. Place 6 oysters on the 4 bottom slices. Top with lettuce, tomato, and pickle; add top 4 slices of bread. Place on individual serving plates. Yield: 4 servings.

NEW ORLEANS OYSTER LOAF

1 (1-pound) loaf unsliced
  French bread
½ cup butter or margarine,
  softened
1 cup yellow cornmeal
¼ cup plus 2 tablespoons
  all-purpose flour
1 teaspoon salt
¼ teaspoon pepper
2 (12-ounce) containers
  Standard oysters, drained
Vegetable oil
Fresh parsley sprigs

Remove crust from ends and sides of bread. Trim off top of bread; discard. Scoop out inside of bread, leaving a 1-inch-thick shell. Spread butter over inside and outside of bread; place on a baking sheet. Bake at 425° for 10 minutes or until crisp.

Combine cornmeal, flour, salt, and pepper in a large mixing bowl. Dredge oysters in cornmeal mixture. Deep fry in hot oil (375°) until oysters float to the top and are golden brown. Drain well on paper towels.

Place oysters in bread loaf. Garnish with parsley. Serve immediately. Yield: 4 servings.

New Orleans Oyster Loaf was once known as the "Peacemaker."

OYSTER PIE RAPPAHANNOCK

1 (12-ounce) container
  Standard oysters, undrained
6 slices bacon
2 cups sliced fresh
  mushrooms
½ cup chopped onion
½ cup chopped green onion
¼ cup all-purpose flour
½ teaspoon salt
¼ teaspoon red pepper
¼ cup chopped fresh parsley
2 tablespoons lemon juice
Biscuit Topping

Drain oysters, reserving ¼ cup oyster liquor. Set aside.

Cook bacon in a large skillet until crisp; drain on paper towels. Crumble bacon and set aside, reserving 3 tablespoons drippings in skillet.

Sauté mushrooms, onion, and green onion in bacon drippings until tender. Stir in flour, salt, and pepper; cook 1 minute, stirring constantly. Stir in oysters, reserved oyster liquor, parsley, and lemon juice.

Spoon mixture into a greased 9-inch pieplate; top with Biscuit Topping. Turn edges under; press firmly to rim of pieplate to seal, and flute. Cut slits in crust to allow steam to escape. Bake at 400° for 20 minutes or until crust is lightly browned. Cut into wedges to serve. Yield: 6 servings.

Biscuit Topping:

1½ cups all-purpose flour
2¼ teaspoons baking powder
¼ teaspoon salt
3 tablespoons butter or
  margarine
½ cup milk

Combine flour, baking powder, and salt in a medium mixing bowl; stir well. Cut in butter with a pastry blender until mixture resembles coarse meal. Sprinkle milk evenly over flour mixture; stir until dry ingredients are moistened. Turn dough out onto a lightly floured surface; knead 4 to 5 times. Roll dough to ½-inch thickness. Yield: pastry for one 9-inch pie.

Off-loading oysters at Baltimore Harbor in the early 1800s.

OYSTER STEW

1 (12-ounce) container
    Standard oysters, undrained
1 quart milk
¾ teaspoon salt
¼ teaspoon pepper
¼ cup butter or margarine
Paprika

Drain oysters, placing oyster liquor in a 2-quart saucepan. Bring to a boil. Add oysters, milk, salt, pepper, and butter. Cook, stirring constantly, until butter melts and oyster edges curl. To serve, spoon into serving bowls; sprinkle with paprika. Yield: 6 cups.

PICKLED OYSTERS

3 (12-ounce) containers
    Standard oysters, undrained
1 cup boiling water
1 medium onion, sliced and
    separated into rings
2 hot red peppers, seeded and
    cut into thin strips
2 teaspoons whole
    peppercorns, divided
2 bay leaves
½ cup cider vinegar
1 teaspoon salt
4 drops hot sauce

Place oysters, oyster liquid, and water in a large Dutch oven. Bring to a boil. Remove from heat; let stand 5 minutes or until edges of oysters curl. Drain oysters in a colander, reserving 1 cup liquid.

Layer half of oysters, onion rings, red pepper strips, peppercorns, and bay leaves in a pint jar. Repeat procedure in a second pint jar with remaining ingredients.

Combine reserved oyster liquid, vinegar, salt, and hot sauce. Pour evenly into jars. Cover with metal lids, and screw bands tight. Refrigerate at least 6 days. Yield: 2 pints.

SCALLOPS

BROILED SCALLOPS

2 pounds fresh scallops
½ teaspoon salt
⅛ teaspoon white pepper
½ cup butter or margarine
1 teaspoon minced garlic
Paprika

Rinse scallops in cold water; drain. Arrange scallops in a single layer in a 12- x 8- x 2-inch baking dish; sprinkle with salt and pepper. Set aside.

Melt butter in a small saucepan. Add garlic; cook over low heat 5 minutes. Pour butter mixture over scallops, stirring to coat well.

Broil scallops 4 inches from heating element 2 minutes; stir well. Broil an additional 2 minutes. Sprinkle with paprika, and serve. Yield: 6 servings.

Two types of scallops important to epicures are found in the bays and estuaries all the way from New England to the Gulf of Mexico. The dainty shallow-water bay scallop has an eye, or edible part, that is only half an inch across. The sea scallop from deeper waters is larger and firmer. Either variety is suitable for use in most recipes, but the bay scallop is somewhat sweeter and more flavorful. Scallops are in season from April to October.

SAUTÉED SCALLOPS WITH GARLIC BUTTER

2 pounds scallops
½ teaspoon salt
¼ teaspoon white pepper
¼ cup all-purpose flour
2 tablespoons butter
3 tablespoons vegetable oil
Lemon wedges
Fresh parsley sprigs
Clarified Garlic Butter

Rinse scallops in cold water; drain well. Sprinkle scallops with salt and pepper; toss gently in flour.

Melt butter in a large skillet over low heat; add oil, stirring well. Add scallops, and sauté 6 to 7 minutes. Transfer scallops to a serving platter or individual serving bowls. Garnish with lemon wedges and parsley. Serve with Clarified Garlic Butter. Yield: 6 servings.

Clarified Garlic Butter:

½ cup unsalted butter
1 teaspoon finely chopped garlic

Melt butter in a 1-quart heavy saucepan over low heat. The fat will rise to the top, and the milk solids will sink to the bottom. Remove saucepan from heat. Skim white froth off top. Strain clear yellow butter, keeping back milk solid sediment. Discard milk solids.

Combine clarified butter and garlic; mix well. Yield: ½ cup.

FRIED SCALLOPS

2 pounds scallops
1 cup all-purpose flour
1 teaspoon salt
½ teaspoon pepper
3 eggs, lightly beaten
½ cup milk
2 cups fine dry breadcrumbs
Vegetable oil
Cocktail sauce (page 126)

Rinse scallops in cold water; drain well. Set aside.

Combine flour, salt, and pepper; dredge scallops in flour mixture. Combine eggs and milk; beat well. Dip scallops into egg mixture. Dredge in breadcrumbs.

Fry scallops in deep hot oil (350°) until golden brown; drain on paper towels. Serve immediately with cocktail sauce. Yield: 6 servings.

VIRGINIA BAKED SCALLOPS

2 pounds fresh bay scallops
2 cups buttery round cracker
  crumbs
¼ cup butter or margarine,
  melted
¼ cup catsup
¼ teaspoon sugar
½ teaspoon salt
⅛ teaspoon pepper
¼ cup sliced green onion
1 tablespoon butter or
  margarine, melted

Rinse scallops thoroughly in cold water; drain well. Combine scallops, cracker crumbs, ¼ cup butter, catsup, sugar, salt, and pepper; stir well. Spoon scallop mixture into a greased 1½-quart casserole or 6 greased 10-ounce custard cups.

Combine green onion and remaining butter; sprinkle evenly over scallop mixture. Bake at 350° for 30 minutes or until lightly browned. Serve immediately. Yield: 6 servings.

SCALLOPS AU GRATIN

1 pound fresh scallops
½ pound fresh mushrooms,
  sliced
¼ cup plus 2 tablespoons
  vegetable oil, divided
1¾ cups milk
2 tablespoons cornstarch
½ teaspoon dry mustard
½ teaspoon Worcestershire
  sauce
½ teaspoon salt
¼ teaspoon white pepper
1 tablespoon sherry
¼ cup fine dry breadcrumbs
¼ cup grated Parmesan
  cheese

Rinse scallops in cold water; drain well. Set aside.

Sauté mushrooms in ¼ cup oil in a skillet until tender. Remove mushrooms; set aside. Reserve drippings in skillet.

Combine milk and cornstarch, stirring well to remove lumps. Stir milk mixture and remaining oil into drippings in skillet. Add mustard, Worcestershire sauce, salt, and pepper. Cook over medium heat, stirring constantly, until thickened and bubbly. Stir in scallops, sautéed mushrooms, and sherry.

Pour mixture into a greased 1½-quart casserole. Sprinkle with breadcrumbs and cheese. Bake at 375° for 25 minutes or until lightly browned. Yield: 4 to 6 servings.

Trade card issued by Hull Vapor Stove Company, 1890, is open to interpretation. Ladies attempt to keep cool despite distractions.

SCALLOPS IN SHELLS

1 pound fresh bay scallops
½ teaspoon salt
¾ cup thinly sliced fresh
  mushrooms
2 tablespoons finely chopped
  onion
¼ cup butter or margarine,
  divided
2 tablespoons all-purpose
  flour
1½ cups milk
2 tablespoons grated
  Parmesan cheese
2 tablespoons sherry
½ teaspoon grated lemon
  rind
¼ teaspoon lemon juice
¼ teaspoon salt
Dash of pepper
¼ cup soft breadcrumbs
1 tablespoon butter or
  margarine, melted
Fresh parsley sprigs
Lemon wedges

Combine scallops and cold water to cover in a large saucepan. Let stand 1 hour. Drain and rinse scallops. Return to saucepan; cover with water. Bring to a boil. Reduce heat; cover and simmer 5 minutes. Drain; sprinkle with ½ teaspoon salt. Cover and set aside.

Sauté mushrooms and onion in 2 tablespoons butter until tender. Stir in scallops. Cover and set aside.

Melt 2 tablespoons butter in a heavy saucepan over low heat; add flour, stirring until smooth. Cook 1 minute, stirring constantly. Gradually add milk; cook over medium heat, stirring constantly, until mixture is thickened and bubbly. Stir in cheese, sherry, lemon rind and juice, remaining salt, and pepper. Cook sauce 1 minute.

Add 1 cup sauce to scallop mixture. Spoon scallop mixture evenly into 4 scallop shells. Spoon remaining sauce evenly over scallop mixture.

Combine breadcrumbs and melted butter; sprinkle evenly over scallop mixture. Bake at 375° for 20 minutes or until lightly browned. Garnish with parsley and lemon wedges. Yield: 4 servings.

Seviche made with tiny bay scallops combined with more good flavors makes an unusual seafood cocktail.

SEVICHE

1 pound fresh bay scallops
1 cup lime juice
1 (4-ounce) can diced green
  chiles, drained
2 medium tomatoes, peeled,
  seeded, and diced
¼ cup grated onion
¼ cup olive oil
1 teaspoon chopped fresh
  cilantro
1 teaspoon salt
Dash of pepper
Avocado slices
Lime slices

Rinse scallops thoroughly in cold water; drain well. Combine scallops and lime juice in a large bowl; cover and refrigerate at least 4 hours. Drain well.

Combine scallops, chiles, tomatoes, onion, olive oil, cilantro, salt, and pepper in a large bowl; stir well. Cover and chill thoroughly. Serve cold in cocktail or sherbet glasses. Garnish with avocado and lime slices. Yield: 6 appetizer servings.

SCALLOP COCKTAIL

1½ pounds fresh scallops
3 lemons, halved
Cocktail sauce (page 126)
Lettuce leaves

Rinse scallops in cold water; drain well. Cook scallops in a skillet over medium heat 3 minutes or until scallops begin to shrivel. Drain and chill.

Cut a thin slice from the bottom of each lemon half so that it will sit flat. Gently remove membranes, leaving shell intact. Fill each lemon half with prepared cocktail sauce; set aside.

Line 6 scallop shells with lettuce. Place a lemon half in center of each shell. Surround lemon halves with equal portions of chilled scallops. Serve immediately. Yield: 6 appetizer servings.

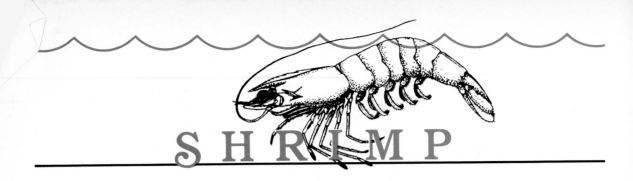

S H R I M P

BROILED MARINATED SHRIMP

2 pounds large shrimp, peeled and deveined
⅓ cup lemon juice
3 tablespoons olive oil
3 tablespoons chopped green onion
2 cloves garlic, minced
½ teaspoon ground saffron
¾ teaspoon salt
¼ teaspoon pepper
¼ teaspoon dried whole thyme
½ cup butter or margarine
Chopped fresh parsley

Place shrimp in a large mixing bowl. Add lemon juice, olive oil, chopped green onion, minced garlic, ground saffron, salt, pepper, and thyme; stir well. Cover and refrigerate 1 hour, stirring mixture occasionally.

Drain shrimp, reserving marinade. Combine marinade and butter in a medium saucepan. Cook over medium heat, stirring occasionally, until butter melts. Set mixture aside, and keep warm.

Place shrimp on a broiling pan. Broil 4 inches from heating element 3 minutes; turn and broil an additional 3 minutes or until done.

Remove shrimp to a warm serving platter, and sprinkle with chopped fresh parsley. Serve warm with prepared sauce of your choice. Yield: about 4 servings.

BOILED SHRIMP

1 (3½-ounce) package shrimp and crab boil
2 bay leaves
2 gallons water
5 pounds shrimp
Cocktail sauce (page 126)

Combine shrimp and crab boil, bay leaves, and water in a large stockpot; bring to a boil. Reduce heat, and simmer 10 minutes. Add shrimp, and cook 4 minutes. (Do not boil.) Drain; rinse in cold water.

Peel and devein shrimp. Serve warm or chilled with cocktail sauce. Yield: 10 servings.

Note: Boiled shrimp may be peeled and deveined for use in any recipe calling for cooked shrimp.

The Phoenix Packing Company of Buras, Louisiana, packaged their extra fancy selected shrimp with this colorful extra fancy label, c.1920. Shrimp is always a good pantry shelf item.

46

GULF COAST SHRIMP BOIL

3 quarts water
2 (12-ounce) cans flat
  beer
2 medium lemons,
  quartered
3 tablespoons sliced
  jalapeño peppers
1 (3½-ounce) package shrimp
  and crab boil
½ cup salt
3 pounds medium shrimp
Cocktail sauce (page 126)

Combine first 6 ingredients in a large stockpot. Bring to a boil; boil 5 minutes. Add shrimp; cook 3 minutes. (Do not boil.) Drain; discard lemon, pepper, and shrimp and crab boil.

Peel and devein shrimp. Serve shrimp hot or chilled with cocktail sauce. Yield: 6 servings or 12 appetizer servings.

SHRIMP FRITTERS

1 cup all-purpose flour
1 teaspoon baking
  powder
1 teaspoon salt
¼ teaspoon pepper
¼ cup milk
2 eggs, beaten
1 pound medium shrimp,
  cooked, peeled, deveined,
  and chopped
2 tablespoons finely
  chopped onion
1 tablespoon chopped
  fresh parsley
⅛ teaspoon hot sauce
Vegetable oil
Cocktail sauce or tartar
  sauce (page 126)

Combine flour, baking powder, salt, and pepper in a medium mixing bowl; stir in milk and eggs. Add shrimp, onion, parsley, and hot sauce; stir well to blend ingredients.

Carefully drop batter by tablespoonfuls into deep hot oil (375°); cook only a few at a time, turning once. Fry until fritters are golden brown. Drain well on paper towels. Serve hot with cocktail sauce or tartar sauce. Yield: 1½ dozen.

Batter-Fried Shrimp (front) and French Fried Shrimp.

BATTER-FRIED SHRIMP

3 cups all-purpose flour,
  divided
¾ cup milk
2 eggs, separated
1 tablespoon olive oil
1 teaspoon salt
2 pounds medium shrimp,
  peeled and deveined
Vegetable oil
Cocktail sauce (page 126)

Combine 2 cups flour, milk, egg yolks, olive oil, and salt in a large mixing bowl; mix well.

Beat egg whites (at room temperature) in a small mixing bowl until stiff peaks form. Gently fold into prepared batter.

Dredge shrimp in remaining flour; dip in batter. Fry in hot oil (375°) until shrimp are golden brown and float to top; drain.

Transfer shrimp to a warm serving platter; serve with cocktail sauce. Yield: 4 to 6 servings.

FRENCH FRIED SHRIMP

2 cups all-purpose flour
½ teaspoon sugar
½ teaspoon salt
1 cup cold water
1 egg, lightly beaten
2 tablespoons vegetable
  oil
2 pounds medium shrimp,
  peeled and deveined
Vegetable oil
Cocktail sauce (page 126)

Combine flour, sugar, salt, water, egg, and 2 tablespoons oil in a large mixing bowl. Stir briskly until smooth. Dip shrimp in batter.

Fry shrimp, a few at a time, in deep hot oil (375°) until shrimp float to the top and are light brown. Drain on paper towels.

Remove to a warm serving platter, and serve immediately with cocktail sauce. Yield: 4 to 6 servings.

Herb Traub's Pirates' House Restaurant in Savannah, famous for seafood dishes.

SHRIMP PIE

6 cups water
1 (3½-ounce) package shrimp and crab boil
1 tablespoon salt
2 pounds large shrimp
1½ cups chopped onion
1 cup chopped green pepper
1 cup chopped celery
½ cup butter or margarine
1 (14½-ounce) can whole tomatoes, undrained and finely chopped
1 teaspoon salt
⅛ teaspoon pepper
2 cups herb stuffing mix
1¼ cups (5 ounces) shredded extra sharp Cheddar cheese, divided
¼ cup plus 2 tablespoons commercial barbecue sauce
¼ cup catsup
1 tablespoon Worcestershire sauce
Hot sauce to taste

Combine water, shrimp and crab boil, and 1 tablespoon salt in a Dutch oven. Bring to a boil; reduce heat, and simmer 2 minutes. Stir in shrimp; return to a boil, and cook 3 minutes. Drain well. Rinse with cold water. Let cool to touch. Peel and devein shrimp; set aside.

Sauté onion, green pepper, and celery in butter in a large heavy skillet until tender. Remove from heat, and set aside.

Combine tomatoes, 1 teaspoon salt, and pepper in a saucepan; cook over medium heat 10 minutes.

Add stewed tomatoes to vegetable mixture in skillet; mix well. Cook over low heat 5 minutes. Add stuffing mix; stir well. Stir in 1 cup shredded cheese; remove from heat. Add barbecue sauce, catsup, Worcestershire sauce, hot sauce, and reserved shrimp; mix well.

Spoon mixture into a 2-quart casserole; sprinkle remaining cheese over top. Bake at 350° for 30 minutes. Serve hot. Yield: 8 servings.

PIRATES' HOUSE SHRIMP PILAU

4 slices bacon
½ cup chopped onion
¼ cup chopped green pepper
1 (14½-ounce) can tomatoes, undrained and chopped
1½ pounds medium shrimp, peeled and deveined
1 cup uncooked regular rice
¾ cup water
½ teaspoon salt
¼ teaspoon pepper
⅛ teaspoon hot sauce

Cook bacon in a large skillet until crisp; drain, reserving 2 tablespoons drippings in skillet. Crumble bacon; set aside.

Sauté onion and green pepper in bacon drippings until tender. Stir in tomatoes; cook over medium heat 2 minutes. Stir in remaining ingredients and reserved bacon.

Pour mixture into a greased 1½-quart casserole. Cover and bake at 350° for 45 minutes or until rice is tender, stirring once during baking. Serve hot. Yield: 6 servings.

SHRIMP GRAVY

1 pound small shrimp, peeled and deveined
1 teaspoon salt
¼ teaspoon garlic powder, divided
⅛ teaspoon pepper
6 slices bacon
¼ cup all-purpose flour
1½ cups chopped onion
1 cup chopped celery
¼ cup chopped green pepper
Hot cooked rice

Combine shrimp, salt, ⅛ teaspoon garlic powder, and pepper in a mixing bowl; mix well. Set aside.

Cook bacon in a skillet until crisp. Drain, reserving drippings in skillet. Crumble bacon, and set aside. Add flour to hot bacon drippings; cook over medium heat, stirring constantly, 10 minutes or until roux is the color of a copper penny. Add onion, celery, and green pepper; simmer 5 minutes.

Add shrimp, remaining garlic powder, and water to cover, stirring well. Cook over medium heat, stirring frequently, until thickened. Add crumbled bacon; stir well. Serve over rice. Yield: 4 servings.

SHRIMP CURRY

¼ cup butter or margarine
¼ cup all-purpose flour
1½ cups milk
1 teaspoon curry powder
½ teaspoon salt
Dash of red pepper
Dash of paprika
¼ cup sherry
1 tablespoon catsup
2 cups peeled and deveined
　cooked medium shrimp
Hot cooked rice
Chopped fresh parsley
　(optional)
Condiments

Melt butter in a large skillet over low heat. Add flour; mix until smooth. Cook 1 minute, stirring constantly.

Gradually add milk, blending until smooth. Cook over medium heat, stirring constantly, until thickened and bubbly. Stir in curry powder, salt, pepper, and paprika; mix well. Add sherry, catsup, and shrimp; mix well. Cook until thoroughly heated.

Serve shrimp mixture over mounds of hot cooked rice; sprinkle with parsley, if desired. Serve with several of the following condiments: (about ¾ cup each) chutney, flaked coconut, chopped hard-cooked egg, salted peanuts, and raisins. Yield: 4 servings.

THE HOMESTEAD SHRIMP CREOLE FRICASSEE

¼ cup shortening
¼ cup plus 2 tablespoons
　all-purpose flour
3 tablespoons chopped onion
3 tablespoons chopped green
　pepper
1½ tablespoons chopped
　celery
3 (8-ounce) bottles clam juice
1½ cups chopped, peeled
　tomatoes
3 pounds medium shrimp,
　peeled and deveined
1 cup sauterne
Salt and pepper to taste
¾ teaspoon minced garlic
1 sprig thyme
3 tablespoons chopped fresh
　parsley
3 bay leaves
Rice Mold

Melt shortening in a large saucepan over medium heat; add flour, and stir until smooth. Cook, stirring constantly, 10 minutes or until roux is the color of a copper penny. Stir in onion, green pepper, and celery; cook until tender.

Add clam juice to vegetable mixture and cook, stirring constantly, until thickened and bubbly. Stir in tomatoes, shrimp, wine, and seasonings; cook 20 minutes over low heat. Remove and discard bay leaves.

Spoon mixture over Rice Mold to serve. Yield: 8 servings.

Rice Mold:

4 cups water
1½ teaspoons salt
2 cups uncooked regular rice
¼ cup butter or margarine,
　melted

Bring water and salt to a boil in a heavy saucepan. Add rice, stirring well. Cover; cook over low heat 25 to 30 minutes.

Grease a 1¼-quart ovenproof ring mold. Pack cooked rice into mold; pour butter over top. Place in a pan of hot water. Bake at 350° for 20 minutes. Loosen edges; unmold onto a serving platter. Yield: 1 rice mold.

The Homestead Shrimp Creole Fricassee, served over a rice mold.

SHRIMP CREOLE

2 medium-size green peppers,
  finely chopped
1 medium onion, minced
¼ cup chopped celery
1 bay leaf
1 teaspoon chopped fresh
  parsley
½ teaspoon salt
¼ teaspoon pepper
⅛ teaspoon red pepper
3 tablespoons butter or
  margarine
2 (16-ounce) cans whole
  tomatoes, undrained and
  chopped
1 pound medium shrimp,
  cooked, peeled, and
  deveined
Hot cooked rice

Sauté first 8 ingredients in
butter in a small Dutch oven
until vegetables are tender. Stir
in tomato; simmer 20 minutes.
Add shrimp; cook over medium
heat until thoroughly heated.
Discard bay leaf. Serve immediately over rice in individual
bowls. Yield: 4 servings.

SHRIMP GUMBO

6 quarts water
1½ tablespoons seafood
  seasoning
1½ pounds medium shrimp
2 tablespoons bacon
  drippings
2 tablespoons all-purpose
  flour
1¾ cups finely chopped onion
2 pounds okra, sliced
1 cup chopped ham
1 (24-ounce) can whole
  tomatoes, undrained and
  finely chopped
1 cup chopped celery
1 cup finely chopped green
  pepper
1 pound lump crabmeat
1 clove garlic, minced
1 teaspoon salt
½ teaspoon pepper
½ teaspoon whole oregano
¼ teaspoon whole thyme
2 bay leaves
Hot cooked rice

Bring water and seafood seasoning to a boil in a large Dutch
oven; add shrimp, and return to

*Blessing of the Shrimp Fleet
on Bayou la Batre, near
Mobile, Alabama. A solemn
and beautiful event.*

a boil. Reduce heat, and simmer
3 minutes. Drain well, reserving
liquid; rinse shrimp with cold
water. Peel and devein shrimp;
chill until needed.

Melt bacon drippings in a 10-
quart stockpot over low heat;
add flour, stirring until smooth.
Cook 1 minute, stirring constantly. Add onion, and sauté
until tender. Add okra and ham;
cook over medium heat, stirring
constantly, 10 minutes. Add
next 10 ingredients; mix well.
Pour 6 cups reserved shrimp liquid into gumbo; simmer, uncovered, for 1 hour, stirring
occasionally (add additional
water, if necessary). Add
shrimp, and cook an additional
20 minutes.

Remove bay leaves; spoon
gumbo into individual soup
bowls over rice. Serve immediately. Yield: about 1 gallon.

SHRIMP MOUSSE

1 (10¾-ounce) can condensed
   tomato soup
1 (8-ounce) package cream
   cheese
2 envelopes unflavored
   gelatin
1½ pounds medium shrimp,
   cooked, peeled, deveined,
   and chopped
1 cup mayonnaise
¾ cup finely chopped celery
½ cup finely chopped green
   onion
½ cup finely chopped green
   pepper
1 teaspoon Worcestershire
   sauce
1 teaspoon lemon juice
Pimiento-stuffed olive slices
   (optional)
Cucumber slices (optional)
Fresh parsley sprigs (optional)
Assorted crackers

Combine soup and cream
cheese in top of a double boiler;
cook over hot water until cream
cheese melts and is well
blended. Remove from heat; cool
slightly. Stir in gelatin; mix
well. Add shrimp, mayonnaise,
celery, green onion, green pepper, Worcestershire sauce, and
lemon juice; mix well.

Pour mixture into a lightly
oiled 5½-cup fish mold. Cover
and chill overnight.

Unmold mousse onto a chilled
serving plate. Decorate fish with
pimiento-stuffed olive slices for
eyes and mouth, and cucumber
slices for gills and tail, if desired. Garnish tray with parsley,
if desired. Serve immediately
with crackers. Yield: 18 to 24
appetizer servings.

Shrimp are usually sold
by count rather than
by grade. Large
shrimp run 16 to 20 per
pound, medium 21 to 25,
and small ones 26 to 30 per
pound. Fresh shrimp are
gray, pink, or brown; all turn
pink when cooked.

PICKLED SHRIMP

2 quarts water
1 (8-ounce) package shrimp
   and crab boil
2 pounds medium shrimp
2 cups water
1 cup tarragon vinegar
2 tablespoons olive oil
2 small red pepper pods
1 small carrot, scraped and
   cut into thin strips
3 cloves garlic
Rind of 1 lemon
1 bay leaf
1 teaspoon whole cloves
½ teaspoon peppercorns

Combine water and shrimp
and crab boil in a large stockpot; bring to a boil. Add shrimp
and cook 3 minutes. (Do not
boil.) Drain; peel and devein
shrimp. Chill thoroughly.

Combine remaining ingre-
dients in a medium saucepan.
Bring mixture to a boil, and boil
5 minutes.

Place chilled shrimp in a 1-
quart jar. Add hot spice mixture; seal jar. Shake well; let
stand 12 hours at room temperature. Store in refrigerator.
(This will keep 2 to 3 days.)
Yield: 1 quart.

SHRIMP PASTE

1½ pounds medium shrimp,
   cooked, peeled, and
   deveined
¾ cup butter, softened
2 tablespoons lemon juice
¼ teaspoon onion juice
½ teaspoon salt
¼ teaspoon red pepper
¼ teaspoon dry mustard
¼ teaspoon ground mace
Assorted crackers

Position knife blade in food
processor bowl; place shrimp in
bowl, and cover with lid. Coarsely grind shrimp. (A meat
grinder may be used instead of
food processor, if desired.)

Combine ground shrimp and
butter in a medium mixing
bowl; stir until well blended.
Add lemon juice, onion juice,
salt, pepper, mustard, and
mace; mix well. Refrigerate several hours. Serve with crackers.
Yield: about 2½ cups.

Note: Shrimp paste may be
spooned into a lightly greased
decorative mold.

*Shrimp Paste can make
a party out of a simple
get-together. Bland
crackers point up the flavor.*

ST. AUGUSTINE SHRIMP

2 quarts water
1 small onion, peeled and quartered
1 lemon, sliced
½ cup celery leaves
3 tablespoons salt
Dash of red pepper
1 bay leaf
1 clove garlic, halved
2 pounds medium shrimp
1 cup finely chopped celery
¼ cup plus 1 tablespoon olive oil
¼ cup finely chopped onion
¼ cup catsup
2 tablespoons lemon juice
1 tablespoon prepared horseradish
1 tablespoon prepared mustard
1 tablespoon chopped chives
1 clove garlic, crushed
Dash of hot sauce
Salt to taste
Leaf lettuce
Black olives
Stuffed egg halves

Combine first 8 ingredients in a large Dutch oven. Bring to a boil. Reduce heat, and simmer 15 minutes. Add shrimp; cook 3 minutes. (Do not boil.) Remove from heat; let shrimp cool in liquid 30 minutes. Drain; discard onion, lemon, bay leaf, and garlic. Peel and devein shrimp.

Combine chopped celery, olive oil, chopped onion, catsup, lemon juice, horseradish, mustard, chives, crushed garlic, hot sauce, salt to taste, and shrimp in a large mixing bowl; stir well. Cover and chill several hours.

Spoon shrimp mixture onto a lettuce-lined platter. Garnish with olives and eggs. Yield: 4 servings or 8 appetizer servings.

St. Augustine, the oldest city in the United States, occupies a peninsula between the Matanzas and San Sebastian Rivers in northeast Florida. Pedro Menéndez de Avilés founded the town on the site of an ancient Indian village on St. Augustine's Day in 1565, near where Ponce de Leon had landed in 1513. After three centuries of turbulence, St. Augustine was ceded to the United States. In 1638 the Spaniards began the stone fort San Marco, now Fort Marion, which was completed 118 years later. Other tourist attractions are the old city gate and the oldest house in America.

SHRIMP REMOULADE

1 cup chopped green onion
½ cup chopped celery
¼ cup chopped fresh parsley
¼ cup chopped dill pickle
1 clove garlic, chopped
2 tablespoons vinegar
1 teaspoon paprika
½ teaspoon salt
¼ teaspoon pepper
2 cups mayonnaise
1 (5¼-ounce) jar Creole mustard
¼ cup vegetable oil
5 pounds medium shrimp, cooked, peeled, and deveined
Leaf lettuce

Place first 9 ingredients in container of an electric blender; cover and process until smooth. Remove cover; continue to process while gradually adding mayonnaise and mustard alternately until mixture is smooth. Continue processing, adding oil in a thin, steady stream. Blend until smooth.

Combine sauce and shrimp in a large bowl. Cover and refrigerate at least 12 hours. Spoon shrimp mixture onto lettuce-lined serving plates. Yield: 10 to 12 servings.

Gulf Bay was another brand of fancy shrimp canned by Phoenix Packing Company of Buras, Louisiana.

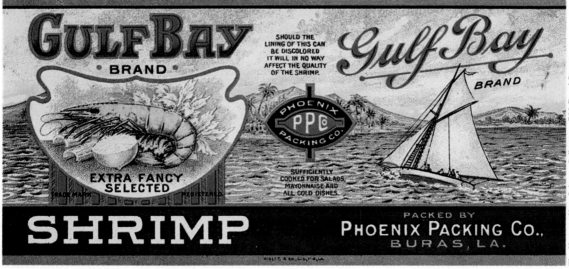

St. Augustine Shrimp, temptingly dressed and garnished.

COMBINATIONS

LOW COUNTRY SEAFOOD CASSEROLE

¾ cup butter or margarine
¾ cup plus 1 tablespoon all-purpose flour
3 cups half-and-half
2 cups (8 ounces) shredded sharp Cheddar cheese
1½ teaspoons salt
½ teaspoon red pepper
1 small onion, grated
¾ cup sherry
2 pounds medium shrimp, cooked, peeled, and deveined
1 pound scallops
1 pound lump crabmeat, drained and flaked
2 (14-ounce) cans artichoke hearts, drained and quartered
2 (8-ounce) cans sliced water chestnuts, drained
½ cup sliced almonds
½ cup grated Parmesan cheese

Melt butter in a Dutch oven over low heat; add flour, stirring until smooth. Cook 1 minute, stirring constantly. Gradually add half-and-half; cook over medium heat, stirring constantly, until thickened. Add Cheddar cheese, salt, and pepper, stirring until cheese melts. Stir in onion and sherry.

Arrange shrimp, scallops, crabmeat, artichokes, and water chestnuts in a lightly greased 3½-quart shallow casserole. Pour sauce over seafood and vegetables; sprinkle with almonds and Parmesan cheese. Bake at 350° for 30 minutes or until lightly browned. Yield: 8 to 10 servings.

SEAFOOD NEWBURG

½ cup butter or margarine, divided
3 tablespoons all-purpose flour
2 cups milk
1 (12-ounce) container Standard oysters, drained
½ pound lump crabmeat
½ pound medium shrimp, cooked, peeled, and deveined
⅛ teaspoon salt
⅛ teaspoon pepper
Dash of hot sauce
¼ cup sherry
8 baked commercial patty shells

Melt 3 tablespoons butter in a heavy saucepan over low heat; add flour, stirring until smooth. Cook 1 minute, stirring constantly. Gradually add milk; cook over medium heat, stirring constantly, until thickened. Remove from heat; set aside.

Melt remaining butter in a large skillet; sauté oysters, crabmeat, shrimp, salt, pepper, and hot sauce 5 minutes or until edges of oysters curl. Stir in white sauce and sherry. Cook 1 to 2 minutes. Spoon mixture evenly into patty shells. Serve immediately. Yield: 8 servings.

Collection of Kit Barry

Trade card for oysters packed by E.B. Mallory, Baltimore, 1890.

BAKED SEAFOOD AU GRATIN

1 medium onion, chopped
1 medium-size green pepper, seeded and chopped
1 cup butter or margarine, divided
1 cup all-purpose flour, divided
1 pound lump crabmeat
4 cups water
1 pound medium shrimp, peeled and deveined
½ pound scallops
½ pound flounder fillets
3 cups hot milk
1 cup (4 ounces) shredded sharp Cheddar cheese
1 tablespoon vinegar
1 teaspoon Worcestershire sauce
½ teaspoon salt
Dash of pepper
Dash of hot sauce
½ cup grated Parmesan cheese

Sauté onion and green pepper in ½ cup butter in a heavy skillet until tender. Stir in ½ cup flour; cook over medium heat 10 minutes, stirring often. Add crabmeat; stir well. Press mixture into bottom of a lightly greased 13- x 9- x 2-inch baking dish. Set aside.

Place water in a large Dutch oven; bring to a boil. Add shrimp, scallops, and flounder; cook 3 minutes. Drain, reserving 1 cup cooking liquid. Set seafood aside.

Melt remaining butter in a heavy saucepan over low heat; add remaining flour, stirring until smooth. Cook 1 minute, stirring constantly. Gradually add milk and reserved cooking liquid; cook over medium heat, stirring constantly, until mixture is thickened and bubbly. Stir in Cheddar cheese, vinegar, Worcestershire sauce, salt, pepper, and hot sauce. Add shrimp, scallops, and flounder; stir lightly.

Spoon seafood mixture over crabmeat mixture; sprinkle with Parmesan cheese. Bake at 350° for 30 minutes or until lightly browned. Serve immediately. Yield: 8 to 10 servings.

BLUFFTON SEAFOOD BOIL

10 quarts water
3 tablespoons salt
1 (3½-ounce) package shrimp and crab boil
6 large potatoes, halved
6 large onions
15 cloves garlic
6 lemons, halved
1 cup vinegar
10 pounds medium shrimp
1 dozen blue crabs, steamed, backs removed, and cleaned
1 dozen ears fresh corn, husks and silks removed
Seafood Cocktail Sauce (page 126)

Place water, salt, and shrimp and crab boil in a 5-gallon stockpot. Bring water to a boil. Add potato halves and onions; return to a boil. Cover stockpot, and cook 20 minutes.

Add garlic, lemons, vinegar, shrimp, crabs, and corn; cook 10 minutes. Remove from heat; cool in pot 10 minutes. Drain carefully.

Transfer seafood and vegetables to a newspaper-covered picnic table. Serve with melted butter and Seafood Cocktail Sauce. Yield: 12 servings.

NEW ORLEANS BOUILLABAISSE

1 cup minced white onion
½ cup chopped shallots
1 teaspoon minced garlic
½ cup butter or margarine
2 (12-ounce) containers Standard oysters, drained
1 cup medium shrimp, peeled and deveined
½ cup fresh chopped lobster
½ cup fresh crayfish tails, peeled
1 tablespoon all-purpose flour
2 cups fish stock (page 132)
1 (14-ounce) can whole tomatoes
1 teaspoon salt
½ teaspoon red pepper
Pinch of powdered saffron
1 (4- to 5-pound) redfish, filleted into 6 equal portions

Sauté onion, shallots, and garlic in butter in a large skillet until tender; add oysters, shrimp, lobster, and crayfish. Cook over medium heat 5 minutes, stirring frequently. Stir in flour, and continue cooking 5 minutes. Add fish stock, tomatoes, salt, and pepper; cook over medium heat 20 minutes, stirring frequently. Stir in saffron; simmer 5 minutes.

Place redfish in a 13- x 9- x 2-inch baking dish. Bake at 350° for 20 minutes or until fish flakes easily when tested with a fork. Place each fillet in an individual serving bowl; pour hot seafood mixture over each fillet. Serve hot. Yield: 6 servings.

Crabbing in North Carolina near Lower Cape Fear, c.1910. Crabbing, so they say, concentrates the mind.

PAELLA

6 whole chicken breasts, split
1 tablespoon salt
2 teaspoons paprika
1 teaspoon pepper
¼ cup plus 2 tablespoons olive oil, divided
½ pound chorizo or Italian sausage, casings removed
½ pound pork, cubed
1 large onion, chopped
1 large green pepper, chopped
6 cloves garlic, crushed
4 cups chicken broth
1 cup Chablis or other dry white wine
4 bay leaves
1 large tomato, chopped
1 teaspoon powdered saffron
2 cups uncooked regular rice
1 (10-ounce) package frozen green peas
1 (14-ounce) can artichoke hearts, drained and quartered
1 (4-ounce) jar chopped pimientos, drained
1 dozen large shrimp, peeled (tails on), and deveined
1 dozen crab claws
1 dozen clams in shells, cleaned
4 fish fillets (about ¾ pound)
Lemon wedges

Season chicken breasts with salt, paprika, and pepper. Brown in ¼ cup olive oil in a large skillet. Drain on paper towels; set aside.

Sauté sausage, pork, onion, green pepper, and garlic in remaining olive oil until meats are browned and vegetables are tender; drain. Set aside.

Combine chicken broth, wine, bay leaves, tomato, and saffron in a stockpot; stir well, and simmer 15 minutes. Add rice and browned meats and vegetables. Cover and cook over medium heat 20 minutes or until liquid is absorbed.

Transfer contents of stockpot to paella pan (or 3½-quart shallow baking dish). Discard bay leaves. Gently stir in peas, artichoke hearts, and pimientos. Add shrimp and crab claws so that tips stand up. Distribute clams and fillets evenly throughout dish. Bake, uncovered, at 350° for 20 minutes or until shrimp are pink. Spoon paella in center of a serving platter; garnish with lemon. Serve immediately. Yield: 12 servings.

HOTEL PONCE DE LEON BROCHETTE OF SHRIMP AND OYSTERS

3 dozen fresh mushrooms
2 tablespoons butter
12 slices bacon
3 dozen large shrimp, peeled and deveined
3 dozen shucked oysters, drained
1½ cups all-purpose flour
1 teaspoon sugar
¼ teaspoon salt
2 eggs, beaten
1 teaspoon vegetable oil
1 cup milk
4 egg whites
Vegetable oil
Orange marmalade

Wash mushrooms; pat dry. Sauté mushrooms in butter in a large skillet 5 minutes; remove from heat, and let cool.

Cut bacon slices in half; cook until transparent but not crisp. Drain and set aside.

Alternate shrimp, oysters, mushrooms, and bacon on wooden skewers. Set aside.

Combine flour, sugar, salt, beaten egg, 1 teaspoon oil, and milk in a large mixing bowl; mix well. Beat egg whites (at room temperature) in a small bowl until foamy. Fold into batter. Dip brochettes into batter.

Fry in deep hot oil (375°) until golden brown. Drain well on paper towels. Serve with orange marmalade. Yield: 6 servings.

Oil magnate Henry M. Flagler was one of the first investors to see the fortune to be made in Florida. When he built the Ponce de Leon Hotel, above, in St. Augustine in 1885-87, it was the first large cast-concrete building in the country. It had artesian well water and four Edison dynamos for lighting, but private baths had to be added later. Business was good; Flagler added the Moorish-style Alcazar Hotel, but after a few years the fickle tourists took their money down to Palm Beach. At left is the Hotel Ponce de Leon Brochette of Shrimp and Oysters.

SALTWATER BOUNTY

The finfish on the other side of the salt barrier from the fresh water species came into its own in the South long after the North had established a fishing industry. Prior to the Revolutionary War, salt cod was used as currency in New England; a Northeasterner obtaining credit made a note of indebtedness not in pounds sterling but in pounds of dried cod or fish oil.

The South remained largely agricultural until around the mid-1700s, when single-cropping tobacco gave way to diversification and we entered the era of the Baltimore Clipper ships. With good salt available at last, the South was able to trade salt fish, salt pork, wheat, and corn in the West Indies for rum, sugar, coffee, and spices.

Close to a quarter million varieties of fish have been identified worldwide; some two hundred species inhabit the Chesapeake Bay alone. The shad, that member of the herring family with the deplorable bone structure, overcame basic unpopularity just by being plentiful. It was said that you had to be out of salt pork to eat shad, but nobody turned down the shad roe. When the shadbush blooms, the shad enter fresh water streams on the East Coast to spawn, able to cross, like the salmon and steelhead trout, from salt to fresh water. Shad season begins in winter in the Deep South, ending in May in the Upper South.

Both the spotted seatrout (weakfish) and redfish rate high on Southern tables. The king and Spanish mackerel are our pick of that huge family, while the connoisseur of finfish heaps compliments on the striped and silver mullet, especially broiled or smoked. The glamorous pompano and red snapper frequent our warmest waters ready to charm the fine-tuned palates of gourmets.

Our most plentiful flatfish, the Southern flounder, ranges from Texas to the Carolinas; shrimp trawlers haul them up in their nets, and folks wade shallow brackish waters to "gig" them at night. Summer flounder (fluke) and winter flounder range from the Chesapeake north.

Lacking space for a catalogue of the South's marine wealth, we'll allow the recipes to carry on the introductions.

Poached Red Snapper in Aspic reposes amid fresh vegetable garnish, antique fish service alongside. Recipe includes ingenious method for removing skin.

BLUEFISH

BAKED STUFFED BLUEFISH

1 (6-pound) bluefish, dressed
½ teaspoon salt
¼ teaspoon pepper
1 tablespoon lemon juice
3 cups sliced fresh
  mushrooms
¾ cup chopped celery
½ cup chopped onion
1 tablespoon olive oil
¼ cup Italian breadcrumbs
1 teaspoon chopped, drained
  pimiento
1 teaspoon seafood seasoning
1 lemon, sliced

Rinse fish thoroughly in cold water; pat dry. Sprinkle cavity with salt, pepper, and lemon juice. Set aside.

Sauté mushrooms, celery, and onion in olive oil in a large skillet until tender. Stir in breadcrumbs, pimiento, and seafood seasoning. Stuff cavity of fish with mushroom mixture. Place fish in a lightly greased shallow roasting pan.

Bake at 350° for 35 minutes or until fish flakes easily when tested with a fork. Carefully remove and discard skin from top of fish. Transfer fish to a serving platter. Garnish with lemon slices. Yield: 10 to 12 servings.

CAPT'N BUDDY'S FAVORITE

1 medium-size green pepper,
  seeded and sliced
1 (4-ounce) jar sliced
  pimientos
2 cups Chablis or other dry
  white wine
1 cup butter or margarine
2 cloves garlic, crushed
1 tablespoon anchovy paste
1 teaspoon dried whole basil
1 teaspoon salt
½ teaspoon pepper
12 bluefish fillets (about 3½
  pounds)

Combine green pepper, pimientos, and wine in container of an electric blender, and process until smooth. Pour mixture into a large saucepan. Add butter, garlic, anchovy paste, basil, salt, and pepper; bring to a boil. Remove from heat; set aside.

Arrange fillets in a single layer in two 13- x 9- x 2-inch baking dishes. Pour half of sauce over fish in each baking dish. Bake, uncovered, at 450° for 25 minutes or until fish flakes easily when tested with a fork. Serve immediately. Yield: 12 servings.

Baked Stuffed Bluefish contains a savory mix of vegetables and Italian-style seasonings.

Trolling for Bluefish, *Currier and Ives lithograph, 1866.*

The bluefish is in season in December in Florida waters, and by May it may be caught as far north as New York. In its feeding habits, the blue ranks with the shark and the piranha; it simply mows its way with its teeth through all kinds of fish and crustaceans. A fish is what he eats, it seems: As the blue ranges northward and eats the oily aquatic foods, its own flesh becomes fattier. For this reason, only the freshest of bluefish should be eaten as it spoils easily. Cooking with an acid offsets oiliness.

SEASIDE POACHED BLUEFISH

2 pounds bluefish fillets
1 medium onion, chopped
2 stalks celery, sliced into thin strips
2 carrots, scraped and sliced into thin strips
2 teaspoons salt
¼ teaspoon pepper

Place fillets in a large skillet; add onion, celery, carrots, and seasonings. Add water to cover, and bring to a boil. Reduce heat; cover, and simmer 8 minutes or until fish flakes easily when tested with a fork.

Remove fish and vegetables to individual serving plates. Serve immediately. Yield: 6 servings.

Note: This recipe yields 4 cups coarsely chopped bluefish for use in a salad, if desired.

GRILLED BLUEFISH

6 (½-pound) bluefish fillets
1 cup commercial barbecue sauce

Place fillets in a wire grilling basket; grill over hot coals 3 to 5 minutes on each side, basting often with sauce. Fish is done when it flakes easily when tested with a fork. Transfer to a serving platter, and serve immediately. Yield: 6 servings.

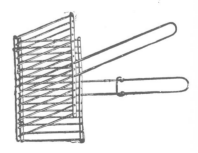

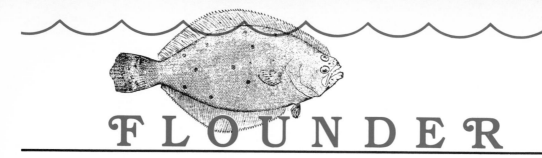

FLOUNDER

Flounder Stuffed with Crab is a favorite in the South.

FLOUNDER STUFFED WITH CRAB

1 (2½- to 3-pound) dressed
   flounder
1 pound lump crabmeat,
   drained
2 teaspoons lemon juice
2 teaspoons chopped fresh
   parsley
1 teaspoon seafood seasoning
1 teaspoon Worcestershire
   sauce
1 medium onion, thinly sliced
2 lemons, thinly sliced
4 slices bacon
2 tablespoons butter or
   margarine
Salt and pepper to taste
Lemon halves
Fresh parsley sprigs

Lay flounder on a cutting board, light side down; slit lengthwise, beginning ¾ inch from head and cutting down center of fish to tail. Make a crosswise slit in flounder near head. Cut flesh along both sides of backbone to tail, allowing the knife to run over the rib bones to form a pocket for stuffing. Set fish aside.

Combine next 5 ingredients in a small mixing bowl, tossing lightly to mix. Spoon mixture into pocket of fish. Top fish with onion and lemon slices. Place bacon over fish across pocket opening. Dot with butter.

Bake, uncovered, at 350° for 30 minutes or until fish flakes easily when tested with a fork. Remove onion, lemon slices, and bacon, and discard. Transfer to a serving platter. Sprinkle with salt and pepper. Garnish with lemon halves and parsley sprigs. Serve immediately. Yield: 4 to 6 servings.

P eople who "don't like fish" will frequently order sole because it "doesn't taste like fish." But unless a restaurant lays claim to serving "Genuine Imported Dover Sole" or "Imported English Sole," that "un-fish" is probably going to be flounder. One reason for the tricky nomenclature is that flounders suffer from such unattractive real names: The witch flounder sells better as gray sole.

FILLET OF FLOUNDER MARGUÉRY

4 flounder fillets (about 3 pounds)
⅔ cup Chablis or other dry white wine, divided
1 teaspoon salt, divided
½ pound fresh mushrooms, sliced
2 tablespoons butter or margarine
3 tablespoons all-purpose flour
2 cups whipping cream
1 pound cooked shrimp, chopped
¼ teaspoon white pepper

Arrange fillets in a buttered 13- x 9- x 2-inch baking pan. Pour ⅓ cup wine over top; sprinkle fillets with ½ teaspoon salt. Bake at 350° for 15 minutes or until fish flakes easily when tested with a fork. Baste every 5 minutes with wine stock in pan. Transfer fillets to a serving platter, and keep warm. Reserve ½ cup wine stock.

Sauté mushrooms in butter in a small skillet until tender; set aside.

Combine reserved wine stock and flour in a large heavy saucepan; beat well with a wire whisk. Place over medium heat, and cook 1 minute, stirring constantly. Gradually add whipping cream; continue to cook over medium heat, stirring constantly, until thickened and bubbly. Remove from heat; stir in remaining wine, sautéed mushrooms, shrimp, remaining salt, and pepper. Pour shrimp-mushroom sauce over fillets, and serve immediately. Yield: 8 to 10 servings.

Fishing from pier of The Breakers Hotel, Palm Beach, 1912.

FLOUNDER FILLETS WITH SHRIMP STUFFING

1 dozen cooked large shrimp, divided
1 small onion, minced
¼ cup chopped green pepper
1 clove garlic, crushed
¾ cup plus 1 tablespoon butter or margarine, divided
¼ cup soft breadcrumbs
1 tablespoon chopped fresh parsley
¾ teaspoon salt, divided
⅛ teaspoon pepper
4 flounder fillets (about 1½ pounds)
3 egg yolks, beaten
2 tablespoons lemon juice
⅛ teaspoon red pepper

Chop 8 shrimp, and set aside. Reserve remaining shrimp for garnish.

Sauté onion, green pepper, and garlic in ¼ cup butter in a medium skillet until onion is tender. Add chopped shrimp, breadcrumbs, parsley, ½ teaspoon salt, and ⅛ teaspoon pepper to vegetable mixture; mix well, and remove from heat.

Spread shrimp mixture evenly over fillets. Roll up each fillet, and place seam side down in a greased 10- x 6- x 2-inch baking dish. Melt 1 tablespoon butter, and brush over fillet rolls. Bake at 350° for 25 minutes or until fish flakes easily when tested with a fork.

Melt remaining ½ cup butter in a small saucepan over low heat. Add beaten yolks, lemon juice, remaining salt, and red pepper; continue to cook over low heat until thickened.

Remove fillet rolls to a warm serving platter. Top with egg sauce, and garnish with reserved whole shrimp. Yield: 4 servings.

FLOUNDER EN PAPILLOTE

Parchment paper
¼ pound fresh mushrooms, sliced
¼ cup plus 2 tablespoons butter or margarine, divided
3 tablespoons all-purpose flour
1 cup milk
2 tablespoons sherry
½ teaspoon salt
¼ teaspoon paprika
4 flounder fillets (about 2 pounds)
½ pound medium shrimp, peeled and deveined

Cut four 14- x 12-inch pieces of parchment paper; cut each into a large heart shape. Fold in half; set aside.

Sauté mushrooms in 1 tablespoon butter in a small skillet until tender. Set aside.

Melt 3 tablespoons butter in a heavy saucepan over low heat; add flour, stirring until smooth. Cook 1 minute, stirring constantly. Gradually add milk, sherry, and seasonings; cook over medium heat, stirring constantly, until mixture is thickened and bubbly. Stir in sautéed mushrooms.

Melt remaining butter; open paper heart out flat, and lightly brush surface with butter.

Place 1 flounder fillet on half of each paper heart; top each with one-fourth of shrimp, and pour mushroom sauce evenly over shrimp. Fold paper edges over to seal securely. Carefully place parchment bags on a baking sheet. Bake at 425° for 15 minutes or until bags are puffed and lightly browned. Place on individual serving plates before cutting an opening in bags. Yield: 4 servings.

BROILED FLOUNDER WITH MUSHROOM-WINE SAUCE

2 pounds flounder fillets
3 tablespoons butter or margarine, divided
2 tablespoons lemon juice
1⅛ teaspoons salt, divided
2 slices bacon, diced
¼ cup chopped green onion
1 small clove garlic, finely minced
½ cup sliced fresh mushrooms
1 teaspoon all-purpose flour
¼ cup catsup
¼ cup Chablis or other dry white wine
¼ cup water

Place fillets in a single layer in a well-greased 13- x 9- x 2-inch baking dish. Melt 2 tablespoons butter; pour butter and lemon juice over fillets, and sprinkle with 1 teaspoon salt. Broil 4 inches from heating element 10 minutes or until fish flakes easily when tested with a fork. (Do not turn.)

Cook bacon in a heavy skillet until crisp; drain bacon pieces, reserving drippings in skillet. Add remaining butter to bacon drippings. Sauté green onion and garlic in drippings until tender. Add mushrooms and flour, stirring until smooth. Cook over low heat 1 minute, stirring constantly. Gradually add catsup, wine, water, and remaining salt; cook over medium heat, stirring constantly, until slightly thickened and bubbly.

Place broiled fillets on a serving platter. Spoon sauce over fillets; sprinkle with reserved bacon. Serve immediately. Yield: 6 servings.

Pictured in the 1901 reprint of R. Lydekker's The New Natural History *are only a few of the many species of flatfish known as flounder.*

BROILED STUFFED FLOUNDER FILLETS

3 slices sandwich bread
¼ cup chopped onion
3 tablespoons chopped celery
2 tablespoons chopped green pepper
1 clove garlic, minced
2 tablespoons butter or margarine
¾ pound lump crabmeat, flaked
3 tablespoons chopped fresh parsley
1 tablespoon chopped pimiento
1 teaspoon hot sauce
¼ teaspoon salt
⅛ teaspoon pepper
6 flounder fillets (about 2 pounds)
Basting sauce (recipe follows)

Place bread in a small bowl; add water to cover. Set aside.

Sauté onion, celery, green pepper, and garlic in butter in a large skillet; add crabmeat, parsley, pimiento, hot sauce, salt, and pepper, stirring well. Drain bread; squeeze any excess water from bread slices. Add bread to crabmeat mixture, stirring until well blended. Cover and simmer over low heat 10 minutes, stirring once.

Place 3 fillets on a rack in a large broiler pan; spoon one-third of stuffing mixture evenly over each fillet. Top with remaining fillets, and secure with wooden picks. Broil 6 inches from heating element 7 minutes on each side or until fish flakes easily when tested with a fork. Baste frequently with basting sauce while broiling. Transfer stuffed flounder to a serving platter, and serve immediately. Yield: 6 servings.

Basting Sauce:

½ cup butter or margarine, melted
¼ cup chopped fresh parsley
¼ cup lemon juice
2 cloves garlic, minced

Combine all ingredients, stirring well. Yield: about ¾ cup.

New York Public Library

Fisherman and catch pose in Florida studio, c.1910.

BATTER-FRIED FLOUNDER

2 eggs, separated
2 tablespoons all-purpose flour
2 tablespoons water
½ teaspoon salt
1 pound flounder fillets, cut into serving-size pieces
¼ cup vegetable oil

Combine egg yolks, flour, water, and salt in a medium mixing bowl; stir well. Beat egg whites (at room temperature) until stiff peaks form; gently fold into yolk mixture.

Dip fillet pieces in batter a few at a time, coating well. Fry in hot oil in a heavy skillet over medium-high heat until lightly browned on both sides. Turn twice during frying process. Drain well on paper towels. Serve immediately. Yield: 2 to 4 servings.

FILLET DE FLOUNDER À L'ORLY

1 (5-ounce) can whole tomatoes, chopped
1 tablespoon plus 1 teaspoon butter or margarine, divided
2 cups water
2 cloves garlic, minced
1 bay leaf, crumbled
1 sprig fresh thyme, minced
1 tablespoon all-purpose flour
1½ teaspoons salt, divided
½ teaspoon pepper, divided
1 egg, lightly beaten
¼ cup milk
1½ pounds flounder fillets
2½ cups soft breadcrumbs
½ cup butter
Fresh parsley sprigs

Combine tomatoes, 1 teaspoon butter, and water in a medium saucepan. Bring to a boil; boil 10 minutes, stirring often. Add garlic, bay leaf, and thyme. Return to a boil; continue to boil until mixture is reduced to 1½ cups. Remove from heat, and mash through a sieve; set aside.

Melt remaining 1 tablespoon butter in a medium saucepan; stir in flour. Cook over medium heat, stirring constantly, until lightly browned. Stir in pureed tomato mixture, ½ teaspoon salt, and ¼ teaspoon pepper. Continue to cook over medium heat, stirring constantly, until sauce thickens. Set aside.

Combine egg and milk in a medium mixing bowl; stir well. Sprinkle fish with remaining salt and pepper. Dip fish in egg mixture, and roll in breadcrumbs. Melt ½ cup butter in a large skillet over medium heat; add fish, and fry until golden brown and fish flakes easily when tested with a fork. Drain on paper towels.

Transfer fish to a warm serving platter, and garnish with fresh parsley sprigs. Serve immediately with reserved sauce. Yield: 4 servings.

FLOUNDER COURT BOUILLON

1 (1¾-pound) dressed flounder
1 cup chopped onion
½ cup chopped green onion
½ cup chopped fresh parsley
¼ cup chopped green pepper
1 clove garlic, minced
2 tablespoons butter or margarine
1 cup tomato juice
½ cup tomato puree
Mushroom Sauce
1 lemon, sliced
¼ cup Chablis or other dry white wine
Hot cooked rice

Drop flounder into boiling salted water; cook over high heat 8 minutes or until fish flakes easily when tested with a fork. Remove fish from water, and cool. Gently flake fish from bones, and set aside, discarding bones.

Sauté onion, parsley, green pepper, and garlic in butter in a large skillet; add tomato juice, tomato puree, and cooked fish, stirring well. Simmer, uncovered, 30 minutes. Stir in Mushroom Sauce, lemon slices, and wine; simmer, uncovered, an additional 10 minutes. Remove from heat, and serve immediately over hot cooked rice. Yield: 6 servings.

Mushroom Sauce:

½ cup sliced fresh mushrooms
3 tablespoons butter or margarine
3 tablespoons all-purpose flour
1½ cups milk
½ teaspoon salt
¼ teaspoon pepper

Sauté sliced mushrooms in butter in a heavy saucepan over low heat until tender. Add flour, and stir until smooth. Cook 1 minute, stirring constantly. Gradually add milk; cook over medium heat, stirring constantly, until thickened and bubbly. Stir in salt and pepper. Yield: about 1½ cups.

GROUPER

BAKED GROUPER

1 (3-pound) dressed grouper
2 tablespoons butter or
  margarine, divided
1 (6-ounce) can sliced
  mushrooms, drained
5 green onions, chopped
1 bay leaf
Pinch of ground thyme
½ cup soft breadcrumbs
1 cup Chablis or other dry
  white wine
Salt and pepper to taste
Fresh parsley sprigs

Rinse fish thoroughly in cold water; pat dry, and place in a 13- x 9- x 2-inch baking dish. Add 1 tablespoon butter, mushrooms, onion, bay leaf, and thyme. Sprinkle fish with breadcrumbs; dot with remaining butter. Add wine to baking dish. Bake at 350° for 1 hour or until fish flakes easily when tested with a fork. Baste occasionally with pan juices.

Remove fish and vegetables to a warm serving platter, discarding bay leaf; sprinkle with salt and pepper to taste. Garnish with parsley. Serve immediately. Yield: 4 to 6 servings.

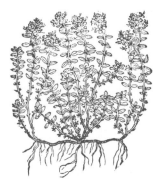

BAKED GROUPER WITH LEMON STUFFING

¾ cup chopped celery
½ cup chopped onion
¼ cup plus 1 tablespoon
  vegetable oil, divided
4 cups toasted bread
  cubes
½ cup commercial sour
  cream
2 tablespoons grated
  lemon rind
¼ cup chopped lemon
  pulp
1 teaspoon paprika
1 teaspoon salt, divided
1 (4-pound) grouper fillet,
  cut with 2 pockets
Lemon twists

Sauté chopped celery and onion in ¼ cup oil in a large skillet until tender; remove from heat. Add toasted bread cubes, sour cream, lemon rind, lemon pulp, paprika, and ½ teaspoon salt, stirring well.

Sprinkle fish with remaining ½ teaspoon salt; stuff pockets of fish with lemon mixture, and place fish in a shallow baking pan. Brush surface of fish with remaining 1 tablespoon vegetable oil. Bake at 350° for 45 minutes or until fish flakes easily when tested with a fork. Transfer fish to a warm serving platter, and garnish with lemon twists. Serve immediately. Yield: 10 servings.

The size of the lemon on this doctored-up postcard could have been a promotion device by the state's citrus industry.

GROUPER ITALIANO

½ cup butter or margarine
1 clove garlic, crushed
6 skinless grouper fillets
  (about 2¼ pounds)
2 cups Italian breadcrumbs
Lemon wedges
Parsley sprigs

Melt butter in a large skillet; add garlic. Remove from heat. Place fish in garlic-butter mixture, turning to coat. Dredge in breadcrumbs.

Place fish on a baking sheet; pour any remaining garlic-butter mixture over fish. Bake at 450° for 20 minutes or until fish flakes easily when tested with a fork. Transfer to a serving platter. Garnish with lemon wedges and parsley sprigs. Serve immediately. Yield: 6 servings.

GRILLED GROUPER

½ cup olive oil
1 tablespoon minced onion
1½ tablespoons grated
  Parmesan cheese
¾ teaspoon dried basil leaves
¾ teaspoon dry mustard
¾ teaspoon dried oregano
  leaves
¾ teaspoon sugar
2 teaspoons salt
¾ teaspoon pepper
¼ cup red wine vinegar
1 tablespoon lemon juice
1 (1½- to 2-inch-thick)
  grouper fillet (about 2
  pounds)
Lemon wedges

Combine olive oil, onion, cheese, basil, mustard, oregano, sugar, salt, and pepper in container of an electric blender; process 30 seconds. Add vinegar and lemon juice; process an additional 30 seconds.

Place fish in a wire grilling basket; grill over hot coals 10 minutes on each side or until fish flakes easily when tested with a fork. Baste frequently with prepared sauce.

Remove fish to a warm serving platter; garnish with lemon wedges. Yield: 6 servings.

GROUPER WITH SPANISH SAUCE

1 large onion, chopped
1 medium-size green pepper,
  chopped
3 cloves garlic, minced
¼ cup olive oil
1 (14.5-ounce) can whole
  tomatoes, undrained
1 (8-ounce) can tomato sauce
2 tablespoons lime juice
1 teaspoon Worcestershire
  sauce
¾ teaspoon salt
¼ teaspoon pepper
⅛ teaspoon ground oregano
1 bay leaf, crushed
1 (2-pound) grouper fillet
¼ cup fine, dry breadcrumbs
2 tablespoons butter or
  margarine
Hot cooked rice

Sauté onion, green pepper, and garlic in olive oil in a large skillet; add tomatoes, tomato sauce, lime juice, Worcestershire sauce, salt, pepper, oregano, and bay leaf, stirring well. Simmer, uncovered, 45 minutes, stirring occasionally.

Place fish in a lightly greased 13- x 9- x 2-inch baking dish, and cover with tomato mixture. Bake at 450° for 10 minutes; remove from oven.

Sprinkle with breadcrumbs, and dot with butter; bake an additional 10 minutes or until fish flakes easily when tested with a fork. Serve immediately over rice. Yield: 6 servings.

GROUPER KABOBS

1 (16-ounce) can pineapple
  chunks, undrained
2 pounds grouper fillets, cut
  into 1-inch cubes
2 medium-size green peppers,
  cut into 1-inch pieces
½ cup soy sauce
¼ cup sherry
2 tablespoons firmly packed
  brown sugar
1 teaspoon ground ginger
1 teaspoon dry mustard
1 clove garlic, minced
Hot cooked rice

Drain pineapple, reserving ¼ cup juice; set juice aside. Alternate pineapple chunks, fish, and green pepper on 6 wooden skewers. Place kabobs in a large shallow dish; set aside.

Combine reserved pineapple juice, soy sauce, sherry, brown sugar, ginger, mustard, and garlic, stirring well. Pour marinade over kabobs; cover and marinate at least 1 hour in refrigerator.

Remove kabobs from marinade, reserving marinade. Grill kabobs over medium-hot coals 15 minutes or until fish flakes easily when tested with a fork. Baste kabobs frequently with marinade. Serve with hot cooked rice. Yield: 6 servings.

POACHED GROUPER

2 quarts water
1 large onion, quartered
1 teaspoon salt
½ teaspoon pepper
2½ pounds grouper fillets, cut
  into serving-size pieces
Fresh parsley sprigs

Combine water, onion, salt, and pepper in a large Dutch oven, stirring well. Bring mixture to a boil; add fish, and cook 15 minutes or until fish flakes easily when tested with a fork. Remove from heat.

Transfer fish and onion to a serving platter using a slotted spoon. Garnish platter with parsley sprigs, and serve with fish stock, if desired. Yield: 6 servings.

rouper Italiano, nice with pasta salad.

HADDOCK

BAKED HADDOCK

1 cup milk
1 tablespoon salt
¾ cup fine, dry breadcrumbs
¼ cup grated Parmesan cheese
¼ teaspoon dried whole thyme
1 (1-pound) haddock fillet, divided into 4 equal portions
2 tablespoons butter or margarine, melted
Paprika
Fresh parsley sprigs
Lemon wedges

Combine milk and salt in a small shallow bowl; stir until salt dissolves. Combine breadcrumbs, cheese, and thyme in a small mixing bowl, stirring until well blended. Dip fish in milk mixture, and dredge in breadcrumb mixture.

Place fish in a buttered 8-inch square baking pan. Pour butter evenly over each portion, and sprinkle with paprika. Bake at 450° for 15 minutes or until fish flakes easily when tested with a fork. Transfer fish to a warm serving platter, and garnish with parsley sprigs and lemon wedges. Serve immediately. Yield: 4 servings.

BAKED HADDOCK WITH LEMON SAUCE

4 haddock fillets (about 1½ pounds)
3 tablespoons butter or margarine, melted
1 cup water
2 tablespoons lemon juice
2 thin slices onion
2 tablespoons butter or margarine
2 tablespoons all-purpose flour
1 egg yolk, lightly beaten
¼ cup whipping cream
½ teaspoon salt
¼ teaspoon pepper
Fresh parsley sprigs
Lemon wedges

Place fish in a well-greased 13- x 9- x 2-inch baking pan; pour 3 tablespoons melted butter over fish. Combine water and lemon juice; pour over fish. Place onion on top of fish. Cover and bake at 350° for 30 minutes or until fish flakes easily when tested with a fork. Transfer fish to a serving platter, and keep warm. Reserve pan drippings.

Melt 2 tablespoons butter in a heavy saucepan over low heat; add flour, stirring until smooth. Cook 1 minute, stirring constantly. Gradually add reserved drippings; cook over medium heat, stirring constantly, until thickened and bubbly. Combine yolk and whipping cream; gradually stir into sauce. Stir in salt and pepper. Cook until sauce is thoroughly heated.

Pour sauce over fish on platter. Garnish with parsley sprigs and lemon wedges. Serve immediately. Yield: 4 servings.

1914 bathing costumes vie for interest with prize catch.

SCALLOPED HADDOCK

1½ pounds haddock fillets,
  cut into serving-size pieces
2 cups coarsely crushed
  crackers
1 teaspoon salt
½ teaspoon pepper
1 tablespoon butter or
  margarine
1 cup milk
1 egg

Lightly grease a 1-quart casse-role. Place half of fillets in dish. Layer with half each of crackers, salt, and pepper. Dot with half of butter. Combine milk and egg, beating well with a fork; pour half of milk mixture over top of casserole. Repeat layering procedure.

Cover and bake at 375° for 30 minutes. Spoon onto serving plates, and serve immediately. Yield: 4 servings.

POACHED HADDOCK

2 pounds skinned haddock
  fillets
1¼ cups milk
¼ cup butter or margarine,
  melted
2 tablespoons all-purpose
  flour
¾ teaspoon dry mustard
¼ teaspoon white pepper
2 hard-cooked eggs, chopped
1 tablespoon chopped fresh
  parsley
¼ teaspoon salt
¼ teaspoon paprika

Place fish in a well-greased large skillet. Pour milk over fish. Cover; bring to a boil. Reduce heat; simmer 8 minutes or until fish flakes easily when tested with a fork. Remove to a serving platter; keep warm. Reserve milk in skillet.

Combine butter, flour, mustard, and pepper. Add to hot milk; cook over medium heat, stirring constantly, until thickened and bubbly. Add egg, parsley, and salt, mixing well. Pour sauce over warm fish; sprinkle with paprika. Yield: 6 servings.

HADDOCK LOAF

2 pounds skinned haddock
  fillets
2 tablespoons all-purpose
  flour
1 teaspoon salt
¼ teaspoon ground mace
½ cup whipping cream
¼ cup butter or margarine,
  melted
Paprika
Fresh parsley sprigs
Lemon slices

Grind fish; combine fish, flour, salt, mace, whipping cream, and butter in a medium mixing bowl. Mix well. Spoon mixture into a greased 9- x 5- x 3-inch loafpan; press mixture evenly into pan.

Place loafpan in a 13- x 9- x 2-inch baking dish; add hot water to dish to a depth of 1 inch. Cover loafpan with greased ung-lazed brown paper. (Do not use recycled paper.) Bake at 350° for 40 minutes or until set. Remove from oven; turn fish loaf out onto a serving dish. Sprinkle with paprika. Garnish with parsley and lemon slices. Slice and serve immediately. Yield: 8 servings.

Haddock Loaf could be served with lemon or egg sauce.

MACKEREL

BAKED SPANISH MACKEREL

2½ pounds Spanish mackerel fillets, cut into 12 equal portions
¾ cup chopped, pitted green olives
3 tablespoons olive oil
½ teaspoon salt
⅛ teaspoon pepper
½ cup chopped, pitted ripe olives
Tomato wedges
Fresh parsley sprigs

Lightly grease a 13- x 9- x 2-inch baking dish. Arrange 6 fillets on bottom. Evenly spoon green olives on each fillet; top with remaining fillets, securing each fillet "sandwich" with wooden picks. Brush surface of fish with olive oil, and sprinkle with salt and pepper. Garnish with chopped ripe olives.

Bake, uncovered, at 375° for 25 minutes or until fish flakes easily when tested with a fork. Transfer to a warm serving platter. Remove wooden picks; garnish with tomato wedges and parsley. Serve immediately. Yield: 6 servings.

Baked Spanish Mackerel: How to dress up a favorite fish.

BROILED SPANISH MACKEREL

2 (1-pound) dressed Spanish mackerel
1 tablespoon olive oil
½ teaspoon salt
¼ teaspoon pepper
Lemon slices
Maître d'Hôtel Butter (page 127)

Rinse fish thoroughly in cold water; pat dry. Rub fish inside and out with olive oil, salt, and pepper.

Place fish on lightly greased rack in a broiler pan. Broil 6 to 7 inches from heating element 5 minutes on each side or until fish flakes easily when tested with a fork.

Transfer fish to a warm serving platter; garnish with lemon slices. Serve immediately with Maître d'Hôtel Butter. Yield: 2 to 4 servings.

The king mackerel can rival its cousin the tuna in size, sometimes weighing up to 100 pounds. Weights of 20 pounds are more common, however, and most cooks like to marinate the king mackerel to subdue the flavor a bit. Owing to its fatty content, it is one of the better candidates for grilling. The Spanish mackerel, averaging 3 to 4 pounds, is smaller and less fatty than the "king" and more subtly flavored.

GRILLED KING MACKEREL

1½ pounds king mackerel
   fillets
8 slices white bread
6 tablespoons butter or
   margarine, softened
2 tablespoons lemon juice
Lemon slices
Watercress

Place fish 4 to 5 inches from hot coals; grill 10 minutes on each side or until fish flakes easily when tested with a fork. Remove from grill; set aside, and keep warm.

Lightly toast bread slices on both sides. Combine butter and lemon juice; beat until smooth. Spread over hot toast; cut toast in half. Serve grilled fish over toast, and garnish with lemon slices and watercress. Yield: 4 servings.

MARINATED KING MACKEREL STEAKS

6 (1-inch-thick) king mackerel
   steaks
¼ cup orange juice
¼ cup soy sauce
2 tablespoons chopped fresh
   parsley
2 tablespoons vegetable oil
1 tablespoon lemon juice
1 tablespoon catsup
½ teaspoon ground oregano
1 clove garlic, minced
¼ teaspoon salt
¼ teaspoon pepper

Rinse fish thoroughly in cold water; pat dry, and place in a large shallow container. Combine remaining ingredients, and pour over fish. Cover and marinate at least 30 minutes, turning fish once.

Remove steaks from marinade; reserve marinade. Place steaks on greased rack in a broiler pan. Broil 5 inches from heating element 4 minutes; turn steaks, and baste with reserved marinade. Broil an additional 4 minutes or until fish flakes easily when tested with a fork. Serve immediately. Yield: 6 servings.

Fisherman's Brand fish label tells how to serve it hot, 1890.

KING MACKEREL STEAKS WITH TOMATO-WINE SAUCE

6 (¾-inch-thick) king
   mackerel steaks
2 tablespoons butter or
   margarine, melted
1 teaspoon salt
⅛ teaspoon pepper
Paprika
Tomato-Wine Sauce

Rinse fish thoroughly in cold water; pat dry. Place on greased rack in a broiler pan. Brush surface of each fish steak with butter, and sprinkle with salt, pepper, and paprika. Broil 5 inches from heating element 5 minutes; turn steaks, and baste with Tomato-Wine Sauce. Broil an additional 5 minutes or until fish flakes easily when tested with a fork. Serve immediately with remaining sauce. Yield: 6 servings.

Tomato-Wine Sauce:

½ teaspoon sugar
4 medium tomatoes, peeled
   and cut into wedges
¼ cup chopped green onion
2 cloves garlic, minced
½ cup plus 2 tablespoons
   butter or margarine,
   divided
½ cup Chablis or other dry
   white wine
2 tablespoons chopped fresh
   parsley
¼ teaspoon salt
⅛ teaspoon pepper

Sprinkle sugar over tomato wedges; set aside. Sauté onion and garlic in 2 tablespoons butter in a large skillet; add wine, and stir until well blended. Simmer, uncovered, 10 minutes, stirring occasionally. Add prepared tomatoes and remaining ingredients; cook over low heat, stirring frequently, until butter melts. Yield: about 2 cups.

MULLET

PECK SMITH'S FRIED MULLET

1½ teaspoons salt
8 (¼-pound) mullet fillets
About 2 cups yellow cornmeal
Peanut oil
Tartar sauce (page 127)

Sprinkle salt over each fish; cover and let stand at room temperature 1 hour.

Dredge fish in cornmeal. Carefully drop fish into deep hot oil (370°). Fry until fish float to the top and are golden brown. Drain well on paper towels, and serve immediately with tartar sauce. Yield: 8 servings.

Suspenseful series of postcards from 1908. Message undoubtedly had a hilarious effect on the recipient.

BAKED MULLET

2 pounds skinless mullet fillets
2 teaspoons lemon juice
Dash of pepper
6 slices bacon
1 large onion, thinly sliced
½ cup soft breadcrumbs
2 tablespoons chopped fresh parsley

Place fish in a single layer in a greased 12- x 8- x 2-inch baking dish. Sprinkle lemon juice and pepper over fish. Set aside.

Cook bacon until crisp; drain well on paper towels, and reserve drippings in skillet. Crumble bacon, and set aside. Sauté onion in bacon drippings over low heat until tender. Place sautéed onion on fish.

Combine reserved bacon,

breadcrumbs, and parsley; sprinkle over fish. Bake, uncovered, at 350° for 25 minutes or until fish flakes easily when tested with a fork. Serve immediately. Yield: 6 servings.

Silver or striped, the mullet is a favorite in every Southern state touched by salt water. In fall, when mullet is plump with roe, smoke cookers are likely to be going full blast all around the Gulf states. Its white flesh is mild with a nutty flavor, while the orange-colored roe may be fried and eaten for breakfast.

6-6-1907

OH! THE BIGGEST FISH
THE OTHER DAY, WHILE WE WERE OUT,
I HOOKED THE LARGEST KIND OF TROUT.
BUT THAT'S NOT HALF—AND IF YOU WISH
I'LL SEND YOU MORE ABOUT THIS FISH.

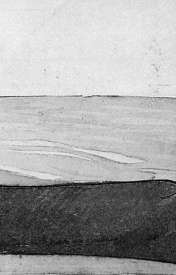

THAT EV
I PLAYED HIM FOR AN HOUR OR MORE
BUT LUCK WAS HARD AGAINST ME, FOR—

MULLET AMANDINE

¼ cup all-purpose flour
1 teaspoon seasoned salt
½ teaspoon paprika
2 pounds mullet fillets, cut
  into serving-size pieces
¼ cup butter or margarine,
  divided
½ cup sliced almonds
2 tablespoons lemon juice
5 drops hot sauce
1 tablespoon chopped fresh
  parsley
Fresh parsley sprigs

Combine flour, seasoned salt, and paprika; mix well. Dredge fish in flour mixture; place in a single layer, skin side down, in a well-greased 15- x 10- x 1-inch jellyroll pan. Melt 2 tablespoons butter, and brush over fish. Broil 4 inches from heating element 10 minutes or until fish flakes easily when tested with a fork. Transfer to a serving platter; set aside, and keep warm.

Sauté almonds in remaining butter in a small skillet until golden brown. Remove from heat; stir in remaining ingredients except parsley sprigs. Pour almond sauce over fish. Garnish with fresh parsley sprigs; serve immediately. Yield: 6 servings.

MULLET FILLETS WITH SHRIMP STUFFING

6 mullet fillets (about 2¼
  pounds)
½ cup lime juice, divided
½ cup chopped onion
¼ cup plus 2 tablespoons
  butter or margarine
4 slices white bread, cubed
⅓ cup plus 2 tablespoons
  water, divided
¼ teaspoon dried tarragon
  leaves
⅛ teaspoon coarsely ground
  black pepper
½ pound medium shrimp,
  cooked, peeled, deveined,
  and chopped
½ teaspoon salt
½ cup tomato juice
2 teaspoons cornstarch
2 tablespoons grated Romano
  cheese

Combine fish and ¼ cup plus 2 tablespoons lime juice in a 13- x 9- x 2-inch baking dish. Cover and let stand 30 minutes.

Sauté onion in butter in a large skillet until tender. Add bread cubes, tossing lightly. Stir in ⅓ cup water, tarragon, and pepper. Remove from heat. Add remaining 2 tablespoons lime juice, shrimp, and salt; mix well, and set aside.

Remove fish from lime juice; drain and discard juice. Return 3 fillets to baking dish. Spread stuffing mixture evenly over fillets; top with remaining fillets. Pour tomato juice around fish. Cover dish with aluminum foil. Bake at 350° for 30 minutes; uncover and continue baking 10 minutes or until fish flakes easily when tested with a fork.

Drain cooking liquid from fish into a small saucepan, leaving fish and stuffing mixture in baking dish. Combine cornstarch and remaining water, stirring to remove lumps. Stir dissolved cornstarch into reserved cooking liquid. Bring to a boil; reduce heat, and simmer 2 minutes or until thickened. Remove from heat.

Pour sauce over fish; sprinkle with cheese. Broil 4 inches from heating element 3 minutes or until browned. Cut stuffed fish in half, and serve immediately. Yield: 6 servings.

Collection of M.E. Warren

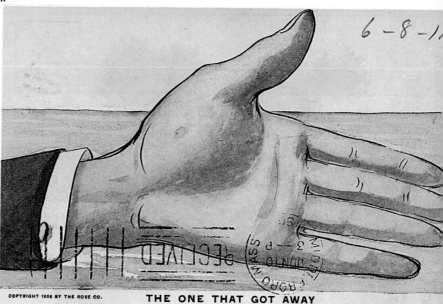

6.-7.-1907

6-8-1.

CAUGHT WAS
MORE JUST NOW—IT'S GETTING LATE
T TIME YOU'LL LEARN THIS MONSTER'S FATE

COPYRIGHT 1906 BY THE ROSE CO.
I HATED MUCH TO SEE HIM DUCK
NEXT TIME I HOPE FOR BETTER LUCK.

THE ONE THAT GOT AWAY
YOU SEE THE CURRENT THERE WAS STRONG
HE MUST HAVE BEEN AT LEAST THIS LONG

GRILLED MULLET

4 (1-pound) whole-dressed
  mullet
Lemon wedges

Rinse fish thoroughly in cold
water; pat dry. Arrange fish in a
wire grilling basket. Grill fish 5
inches from medium-hot coals
10 minutes on each side or until
fish flakes easily when tested
with a fork. Remove to a warm
serving platter; serve with
lemon wedges. Yield: 4 servings.

POACHED MULLET

½ small onion, sliced
2 tablespoons lemon juice
10 whole cloves
¼ teaspoon salt
¼ teaspoon pepper
⅛ teaspoon red pepper
1½ pounds mullet fillets
Lemon wedges

Add water to a large skillet to a
depth of 1 inch. Add first 6 ingredients; mix well, and bring to
a boil. Reduce heat; cover and
simmer 10 minutes. Add fish;
cover and simmer 8 minutes or
until fish flakes easily when
tested with a fork.

Transfer to a warm serving
platter; discard cooking liquid.
Garnish fish with lemon
wedges. Serve immediately.
Yield: 4 servings.

*Smoked Mullet is reason
enough to own a smoker;
choice smoke flavors are
sweet bay and hickory.*

SMOKED MULLET

1 gallon water
1 cup salt
1 (3½-ounce) package shrimp
  and crab boil
6 (¾-pound) whole-dressed
  mullet
½ pound hickory chips,
  soaked in water

Combine water, salt, and
shrimp and crab boil in a large
bowl; stir well to blend seasonings. Rinse fish thoroughly in
cold water; place in brine mixture. Cover; refrigerate 30 minutes, stirring occasionally.

Prepare charcoal fire in
smoker; let burn 10 to 15 minutes. Drain water from hickory
chips to fill water pan half full.
Sprinkle hickory chips over
gray-white coals. Place water
pan in smoker. Heavily grease
wire food rack; place on lowest
shelf in smoker.

Remove fish from brine; rinse
thoroughly in cold water, and
pat dry. Arrange fish on food
rack; cover smoker with lid, and
open vent slightly to keep smoke
and air circulating. Smoke fish
1½ hours or until fish flakes
easily when tested with a fork
and is golden brown. Transfer
fish to a serving platter, and
serve. Yield: 6 to 8 servings.

FLORIDA'S MULLET STEW

1½ cups chopped celery
½ cup chopped onion
1 clove garlic, minced
¼ cup butter or margarine
1 (28-ounce) can whole
  tomatoes, undrained
1 (8-ounce) can tomato sauce
2 teaspoons salt
½ teaspoon paprika
½ teaspoon chili powder
¼ teaspoon pepper
1 (7-ounce) package spaghetti
2 cups boiling water
2 pounds mullet fillets, cut
  into 1-inch pieces
Grated Parmesan cheese

Sauté celery, onion, and garlic
in butter in a large Dutch oven
until tender. Add tomatoes, tomato sauce, and seasonings,
mixing well. Bring to a boil. Reduce heat; cover and simmer 20
minutes.

Add spaghetti and boiling
water; mix well. Cover and simmer 10 minutes or until spaghetti is almost tender. Add
fish; cover and simmer 10 minutes or until fish flakes easily
when tested with a fork.

Spoon stew into individual
serving bowls; sprinkle with
cheese. Serve immediately.
Yield: about 2½ quarts.

POMPANO

POMPANO EN PAPILLOTE

Parchment paper
3 cups water
1¼ teaspoons salt, divided
¼ teaspoon dried whole thyme
1 bay leaf
1 lemon, sliced
6 pompano fillets (about 2 pounds)
1 onion, minced
2 tablespoons butter or margarine
3 tablespoons all-purpose flour
2 egg yolks
1 cup peeled, deveined, and cooked medium shrimp, chopped
½ cup lump crabmeat
6 medium mushrooms, sliced

Cut six 14- x 12-inch pieces of parchment paper; cut each into a large heart shape. Fold in half; open out flat, and lightly butter exposed surface. Set aside.

Combine water, 1 teaspoon salt, thyme, bay leaf, and lemon slices in a large Dutch oven; bring to a boil. Add fillets; reduce heat and simmer, uncovered, 15 minutes or until fish flakes easily when tested with a fork. Remove fillets from fish stock; set aside. Strain stock into a 2-cup glass measure; add water to yield 1½ cups. Set stock aside; discard bay leaf and lemon slices.

Sauté onion in butter in Dutch oven over low heat until tender. Gradually add flour, stirring until well blended. Cook 1 minute, stirring constantly. Gradually add reserved fish stock; cook over medium heat, stirring constantly, until slightly thickened. Gradually stir one-fourth hot mixture into yolks; add to remaining hot mixture, stirring constantly. Stir in remaining salt, shrimp, crabmeat, and mushrooms.

Place one fillet on half of each paper heart; top each with ½ cup shrimp mixture. Fold paper edges over to seal securely. Carefully place parchment bags on baking sheets. Bake at 400° for 10 minutes or until bags are puffed and lightly browned.

Transfer bags to serving plates. Cut an opening in bags, and serve. Yield: 6 servings.

From North Carolina, around Florida, and into the Gulf of Mexico, the pompano lords it over less pricey saltwater delicacies. It endears itself to fishermen by its antics, appearing to dance on the water around a boat, even sometimes hopping aboard. Pompano are at their best in Florida from fall to spring.

A Louisiana pompano dinner by Alfred R. Waud, c.1871.

The Historic New Orleans Collection, 533 Royal Street

Market Street in Charleston, *an oil by C.J. Hamilton, 1872.*

HENRY'S RESTAURANT POMPANO À LA GHERARDI

6 (¾- to 1-pound) dressed
  pompano
1 teaspoon salt
½ teaspoon pepper
Shrimp and Crabmeat Stuffing
18 small shrimp, cooked,
  peeled, and deveined
¼ cup plus 2 tablespoons
  chopped pimiento-stuffed
  olives
3 slices bacon, halved and
  cooked until limp

Rinse fish thoroughly in cold water; pat dry. Lay fish on a cutting board; slit side of fish lengthwise, beginning ¾ inch from head and cutting down center of fish to tail. Cut flesh away from bone down both sides of backbone to the tail, allowing the knife to run over the rib bones to form a pocket for stuffing.

Sprinkle fish with salt and pepper. Stuff each fish equally with Shrimp and Crabmeat Stuffing. Place 3 shrimp over each pocket opening; top each fish with 1 tablespoon chopped olives and bacon half.

Place stuffed fish in 2 greased 13- x 9- x 2-inch baking dishes; cover with aluminum foil. Bake at 400° for 20 minutes or until fish flakes easily when tested with a fork. Transfer fish to a serving dish. Serve immediately. Yield: 6 servings.

Shrimp and Crabmeat Stuffing:

1 cup chopped green onion
¼ cup chopped fresh parsley
½ cup butter or margarine
8 slices white bread, cubed
1 pound cooked medium
  shrimp, peeled, deveined,
  and chopped
½ pound lump crabmeat,
  drained
¼ cup sherry
1 egg, beaten
1 teaspoon salt
¼ teaspoon pepper

Sauté onion and parsley in butter in a large skillet until onion is tender. Add bread cubes, stirring to coat. Stir in remaining ingredients. Yield: about 3 cups.

WINE-BAKED POMPANO IN SAUCE

4 (1-pound) dressed pompano
½ teaspoon salt
¼ teaspoon pepper
1 large onion, chopped
2 sprigs fresh parsley, chopped
¼ teaspoon dried whole thyme
1 bay leaf, crushed
1 cup Chablis or other dry white wine
3 tablespoons butter or margarine, divided
2 tablespoons all-purpose flour
6 medium tomatoes, peeled and finely chopped
½ cup chopped fresh mushrooms
½ cup cracker crumbs
Lemon wedges

Rinse fish thoroughly in cold water; pat dry. Rub fish with salt and pepper; set aside.

Spread onion, parsley, thyme, and bay leaf evenly in bottom of a lightly greased 13- x 9- x 2-inch baking dish. Place fish on top of vegetables; pour wine over top. Bake, uncovered, at 350° for 20 minutes.

Melt 2 tablespoons butter in a small saucepan over low heat; add flour, stirring until smooth. Cook over medium heat until lightly browned. Add tomatoes and mushrooms, mixing well; simmer 10 minutes.

Pour sauce over fish; cover with cracker crumbs. Dot with remaining butter. Bake at 350° an additional 10 minutes or until fish flakes easily when tested with a fork.

Garnish fish with lemon wedges; serve immediately. Yield: 4 servings.

POMPANO JACQUES LATOUR

4 pompano fillets (about 1½ pounds)
1 cup milk
½ cup all-purpose flour
½ teaspoon salt
⅛ teaspoon pepper
Peanut oil
¼ cup butter or margarine
1 tablespoon lemon juice
2 tablespoons chopped fresh parsley
Cucumber slices

Place fillets in a shallow pan; pour milk over fillets. Cover and refrigerate 10 minutes, turning once. Combine flour, salt, and pepper, stirring well. Drain fillets; dredge in flour mixture.

Heat ¼ inch oil in a large skillet. Add fillets; cook 3 minutes on each side or until browned, turning once. Transfer fillets to a serving platter; set aside, and keep warm.

Melt butter in a small skillet over low heat; cook, stirring frequently, until butter is browned. Remove from heat, and stir in lemon juice. Immediately pour butter mixture over fillets; sprinkle with parsley, and garnish with cucumber slices. Serve immediately. Yield: 4 servings.

A successful fishing expedition at Lake Sabine, Texas, 1921.

K.R. Zenos, Sr., copy courtesy of University of Texas Institute of Texan Culture

POMPANO AMANDINE

1 cup all-purpose flour
1 teaspoon salt
½ teaspoon pepper
6 pompano fillets (about 2 pounds)
½ cup butter or margarine, divided
¼ cup sliced almonds
2 tablespoons lemon juice
Lemon slices

Combine flour, salt, and pepper in a large bowl; mix well. Dredge fillets in mixture.

Heat ¼ cup butter in a large skillet over medium heat. Add fillets, and cook 3 minutes on each side or until fish flakes easily when tested with a fork. Transfer to a warm serving platter; keep warm.

Combine remaining butter and almonds in skillet. Cook over medium heat until butter is browned.

Sprinkle fillets with lemon juice. Pour butter-almond mixture over top. Garnish with lemon slices; serve immediately. Yield: 6 servings.

BROILED POMPANO

2 (1-pound) dressed pompano
2 teaspoons olive oil
¾ teaspoon salt, divided
½ teaspoon paprika
½ cup butter
1 tablespoon lemon juice
1 sprig fresh parsley, chopped
¼ teaspoon white pepper
Lemon slices

Rinse fish thoroughly in cold water; pat dry. Rub fish with oil, ½ teaspoon salt, and paprika; place on well-greased rack in a broiler pan. Broil fish 5 to 6 inches from heating element 5 minutes; turn fish, and continue broiling an additional 5 minutes or until fish flakes easily when tested with a fork. Remove fish to a serving platter, and keep warm.

Combine butter, lemon juice, parsley, remaining salt, and pepper in a small saucepan. Cook over low heat until butter melts, stirring occasionally.

Pour butter sauce over reserved fish. Garnish with lemon slices, and serve immediately. Yield: 2 servings.

Broiled Pompano:
The seasonings are kept simple to point up the subtle flavor of the fish.

REDFISH

MISSISSIPPI SOUND BAKED STUFFED REDFISH

1 (5- to 6-pound) dressed redfish
1 large onion, chopped
1 small green pepper, chopped
2 cloves garlic, minced
2 tablespoons chopped fresh parsley
1 tablespoon chopped celery
1 tablespoon shortening
1 pound medium shrimp, peeled and deveined
1 (12-ounce) container Standard oysters, drained
1 bay leaf
1 teaspoon salt
¼ teaspoon pepper
Dash of ground thyme
4 slices bread, cubed and toasted
Creole Sauce
Green pepper rings
Lemon slices

Rinse fish thoroughly in cold water, and pat dry. Place fish in an aluminum foil-lined shallow baking pan.

Sauté onion, green pepper, garlic, parsley, and celery in shortening in a large skillet until tender. Add shrimp, oysters, bay leaf, and seasonings; cook over medium heat, stirring constantly, 5 minutes or until shrimp turns pink. Discard bay leaf. Stir in bread cubes.

Place stuffing in fish cavity; secure with skewers or wooden picks. Pour Creole Sauce over fish. Bake, uncovered, at 350° for 40 minutes or until fish flakes easily when tested with a fork. Transfer to a serving platter. Garnish with green pepper and lemon. Yield: 6 servings.

Creole Sauce:

2 large onions, chopped
1 large green pepper, chopped
2 cloves garlic, minced
2 bay leaves
2 tablespoons chopped fresh parsley
Dash of ground thyme
1 tablespoon shortening
1 tablespoon all-purpose flour
1 (14½-ounce) can tomatoes, undrained and chopped

Sauté first 6 ingredients in shortening in a large skillet until vegetables are tender. Stir in flour; cook over medium heat 2 to 3 minutes. Add tomatoes; cook 10 minutes over medium heat, stirring occasionally. Remove and discard bay leaves. Yield: about 2½ cups.

Young redfish in Southern waters are best harvested in the fall when they are feeding on crab and shrimp. Baked redfish is a favorite dish in the North or South. But unique to the Deep South is the conception of redfish as the basis for a thick, rich court bouillon. Where the weather is hot and cooking a passion, the faint-flavored broth others call court bouillon is, well, foreign. "Cubion" is the pronunciation, and it traditionally begins with a roux.

A fish peddler on his rounds in Mobile, Alabama, c.1895.

Armitstead/Mobile Museum, University of South Alabama Photo Archives

Luke and Malynda Morgan

COURT BOUILLON OF REDFISH

½ cup vegetable oil
1 cup all-purpose flour
3 medium-size green peppers, chopped
2 large onions, chopped
3 stalks celery, chopped
2 cloves garlic, minced
3 (14-ounce) cans tomatoes, undrained
1 cup fish stock (page 132) or water
2 bay leaves, crushed
1 clove garlic, minced
1 tablespoon chopped fresh parsley
2 teaspoons salt
¼ teaspoon red pepper
¼ teaspoon ground allspice
2 thin slices lemon
4 pounds redfish fillets, cut into bite-size pieces
Hot cooked rice
Chopped green onion
Lemon wedges

Combine oil and flour in a large stockpot; cook over medium heat 30 minutes or until roux is the color of a copper penny, stirring frequently.

Stir in green pepper, onion, celery, and garlic; cook, stirring frequently, 15 minutes or until vegetables are tender. Add tomatoes; cook, uncovered, over low heat 1 hour or until oil begins to separate around edge of stockpot; stir occasionally.

Stir in next 8 ingredients; cook, uncovered, 30 minutes, stirring occasionally. Add fish, and cook 20 minutes or until fish flakes easily when tested with a fork.

Serve over hot cooked rice in individual serving bowls. Garnish with chopped green onion and lemon wedges. Yield: 10 to 12 servings.

GULF CITY FRIED REDFISH

2¼ pounds redfish fillets, cut into 6 equal portions
1½ teaspoons salt
½ teaspoon pepper
1 cup cornmeal
Vegetable oil or lard
Sauce (recipe follows)

Sprinkle fish with salt and pepper; dredge in cornmeal. Fry in deep hot oil (375°) until fish float to the top and are golden brown. Drain on paper towels.

Arrange fish around edge of a warm serving platter. Place sauce in a small bowl in center of platter. Serve immediately. Yield: 6 servings.

Sauce:

6 hard-cooked egg yolks
1 tablespoon vegetable oil
1 tablespoon Worcestershire sauce
1 tablespoon prepared mustard
1 teaspoon salt
½ cup catsup
½ cup vinegar
2 tablespoons chopped dill pickle

Combine first 5 ingredients in a small mixing bowl, blending until smooth. Stir in catsup, vinegar, and chopped dill pickle. Yield: 1¾ cups.

REDFISH ASPIC

1 (2-pound) dressed redfish
1 medium onion, sliced
1 teaspoon salt
½ teaspoon pepper
2 envelopes unflavored gelatin
2 stalks celery, cleaned and chopped
1 medium-size green pepper, chopped
1 green onion, chopped
1 teaspoon chopped fresh parsley
1 tablespoon lemon juice
½ teaspoon prepared mustard
½ teaspoon Worcestershire sauce
Fresh parsley sprigs
Lemon wedges
Mayonnaise

Rinse fish thoroughly in cold water; pat dry. Place fish in a large stockpot; add sliced onion, salt, pepper, and water to cover. Bring to a boil. Reduce heat, and cook 15 minutes or until fish flakes easily when tested with a fork.

Remove fish to a cutting board; set aside. Strain fish stock, reserving 1 quart; discard onion. Add gelatin to reserved stock; cook over medium heat until gelatin dissolves. Chill until consistency of unbeaten egg white.

Remove and discard skin of fish; flake fish from bone, discarding bone. Combine flaked fish and next 7 ingredients in a medium mixing bowl; mix well, and fold into gelatin mixture. Spoon into a lightly greased 5½-cup mold; chill until set.

Unmold onto a serving platter. Garnish with parsley sprigs and lemon wedges. Slice and serve with a dollop of mayonnaise. Yield: 10 servings.

S A L M O N

SMOKED SALMON

1 (5½-pound) dressed salmon
Salt
Hickory chips, soaked in
   water
Assorted crackers

Rinse fish thoroughly in cold water; pat dry. Rub entire surface of fish with salt; let stand at room temperature 1 hour.

Prepare charcoal fire in smoker; let burn 10 to 15 minutes. Sprinkle wet hickory chips over gray-white coals. Place water pan in smoker, and fill with hot water.

Lightly grease food rack, and place on appropriate shelf in smoker. Place salmon on rack; cover smoker with lid, and cook 3½ hours or until fish flakes easily when tested with a fork. Chill thoroughly; remove skin, and discard. Serve salmon with assorted crackers. Yield: 20 to 24 appetizer servings.

GRILLED SALMON STEAKS

4 (1-inch-thick) salmon
   steaks
½ cup butter or margarine,
   melted
Juice of 1 lemon
½ teaspoon salt
¼ teaspoon white pepper
1½ teaspoons chopped fresh
   dill

Rinse steaks thoroughly in cold water; drain and pat dry. Place steaks in a wire grilling basket. Combine butter, lemon juice, salt, and pepper; stir well.

Grill steaks over medium coals 10 minutes on each side or until fish flakes easily when tested with a fork. Baste often with butter mixture, reserving a small amount for sauce.

Add dill to remaining butter mixture; stir well. Serve steaks with dill-butter sauce. Yield: 4 servings.

CREAMED SALMON

2 tablespoons butter or
   margarine
2 tablespoons all-purpose
   flour
2 cups milk
¼ teaspoon salt
⅛ teaspoon pepper
1 (15½-ounce) can red
   salmon, drained and flaked
2 hard-cooked eggs, chopped
1 cup soft bread cubes

Melt butter in a heavy saucepan over low heat; add flour, stirring until smooth. Cook 1 minute, stirring constantly. Gradually add milk; cook over medium heat, stirring constantly, until thickened and bubbly. Stir in salt and pepper.

Layer half of salmon and egg in a lightly greased 1-quart casserole; pour half of white sauce evenly over top. Repeat procedure with remaining salmon, egg, and white sauce; sprinkle bread cubes over top.

Bake at 350° for 25 minutes or until bubbly and lightly browned. Yield: 4 servings.

Indian cooking method, illustrated by John White, c.1585.

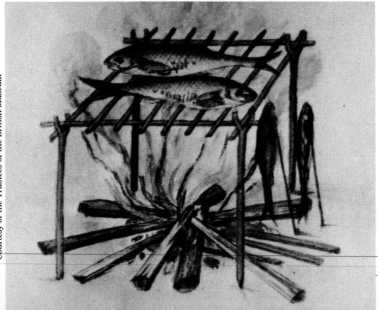

When she wrote, "Salmon . . . requires as much boiling as meat, that is, a quarter of an hour for every pound," Eliza Leslie was passing along the current wisdom of the 1850s. Today the high-heat, quick-time method in use calls for 10 minutes per inch of maximum thickness.

SALMON MOUSSE

1 (15½-ounce) can red
  salmon, undrained
2 envelopes unflavored
  gelatin
1 cup chopped onion
½ cup mayonnaise
½ cup commercial sour
  cream
2 tablespoons lemon juice
1 teaspoon garlic salt
¼ teaspoon dried whole
  dillweed
¼ teaspoon white pepper
4 sprigs fresh parsley
Aspic (recipe follows)
Cooked shell pasta
Green onions, blanched and
  cut into strips
Paprika
Assorted crackers

Drain salmon, reserving liquid; add water to salmon liquid to yield ½ cup. Combine salmon liquid and gelatin in a small saucepan; cook over medium heat, stirring constantly, until gelatin dissolves. Remove from heat, and set aside.

Remove skin and bones from salmon, and discard; flake salmon.

Place gelatin mixture, salmon, onion, mayonnaise, sour cream, lemon juice, garlic salt, dillweed, pepper, and parsley in container of an electric blender; process until smooth. Pour mixture into a lightly oiled 5-cup fish mold. Chill until firm.

Unmold onto a serving tray. Garnish with aspic, cooked pasta, and green onion strips; sprinkle with paprika as desired. Serve with assorted crackers. Yield: 18 to 24 appetizer servings.

Note: Recipe may also be prepared in a food processor. Position knife blade in processor bowl; add ingredients. Process until smooth, and proceed as directed.

Aspic:

2 envelopes unflavored
  gelatin
2½ cups water

Soften gelatin in water in a small saucepan; cook over medium heat, stirring constantly, until gelatin dissolves. Pour mixture into a lightly oiled 15- x 10- x 1-inch jellyroll pan; chill until firm. Cut into ½-inch squares. Turn out of pan. Use to garnish Salmon Mousse. Yield: about 2 cups.

SALMON CROQUETTES

1 (15½-ounce) can pink
  salmon, drained and flaked
3 eggs, beaten
1½ cups crushed crackers
½ teaspoon salt
¼ teaspoon red pepper
Vegetable oil
Cocktail sauce (page 126)

Combine salmon, eggs, cracker crumbs, salt, and pepper in a medium mixing bowl; mix well. Shape mixture into 12 croquettes. Fry in deep hot oil (375°) until golden brown. Drain well on paper towels. Serve immediately with cocktail sauce. Yield: 1 dozen.

Salmon Mousse, garnished, for a stunning party presentation.

SEATROUT

HOTEL CHAMBERLAIN BAKED SEATROUT

8 (½-pound) dressed seatrout
1 teaspoon salt
½ teaspoon pepper
1 cup finely chopped onion
¼ cup plus 2 tablespoons butter or margarine, divided
1 cup Chablis or other dry white wine
2 tablespoons chopped fresh parsley
½ cup Hollandaise Sauce (page 128)
Fresh parsley sprigs

Rinse fish thoroughly in cold water, and pat dry. Sprinkle fish with salt and pepper; place in a well-greased 12- x 8- x 2-inch baking dish. Sprinkle onion evenly over top of fish. Melt ¼ cup butter, and pour over fish. Add wine to baking dish.

Bake, uncovered, at 350° for 20 minutes or until fish flakes easily when tested with a fork, basting occasionally with pan drippings. Remove fish to a serving platter, and keep warm; reserve pan drippings.

Place reserved pan drippings in a medium saucepan. Cook over medium heat until mixture is reduced by half; remove from heat. Stir in remaining butter, chopped parsley, and Hollandaise Sauce; mix well. Pour sauce over fish; garnish with parsley sprigs, and serve immediately. Yield: 8 servings.

Hotel Chamberlain Baked Seatrout in a flavor-rich wine sauce.

Proper fish parlance demands that we differentiate between sea trout (two words) and seatrout (one word). The sea trout is like the salmon in that it is anadromous: It goes from salt water to fresh and is rare on the East Coast. What Southerners have in abundance is the seatrout, usually called by the off-putting name "weakfish," a relative of the drum. The name may stem from its fragile mouth that easily tears away from the hook.

1912 postcard of Hotel Chamberlain looking formidably foursquare, in Old Point, Virginia.

FLORIDA SEATROUT

6 (¾-pound) dressed seatrout
¼ cup butter or margarine, softened
1 hard-cooked egg, finely chopped
3 tablespoons chopped fresh parsley
1 tablespoon diced pimiento
½ teaspoon salt, divided
⅛ teaspoon cracked black pepper
½ cup all-purpose flour
3 tablespoons vegetable oil
Lime slices

Rinse fish thoroughly in cold water; pat dry, and set aside.

Cream butter in a small mixing bowl; stir in egg, parsley, pimiento, ¼ teaspoon salt, and pepper. Set aside.

Combine flour and remaining salt in a large mixing bowl; stir well. Dredge fish in flour mixture. Place fish on well-greased rack in a broiler pan; brush with oil. Broil fish 3 inches from heating element 8 minutes or until fish flakes easily when tested with a fork.

Transfer fish to a warm serving platter; spread each with reserved butter mixture. Garnish with lime slices; serve immediately. Yield: 6 servings.

PAN-FRIED SEATROUT

4 (½-pound) dressed seatrout
1 teaspoon salt
¼ teaspoon pepper
½ cup all-purpose flour
2 eggs, beaten
1 cup cornmeal
½ cup butter or margarine
½ cup vegetable oil
Lemon slices
Remoulade Sauce (page 127)

Rinse fish thoroughly in cold water; pat dry. Sprinkle fish with salt and pepper. Roll fish in flour; dip in egg, and dredge in cornmeal.

Heat butter and oil in a large skillet over medium-high heat. Add fish, and cook until golden brown, turning once. (Fish is done when it flakes easily when tested with a fork.) Drain well on paper towels. Transfer fish to a serving platter, and garnish with lemon slices. Serve with Remoulade Sauce. Yield: 2 to 4 servings.

SEATROUT MEUNIÈRE

4 (½-pound) whole-dressed seatrout
1 teaspoon salt
½ teaspoon pepper
½ cup all-purpose flour
¾ cup butter or margarine, divided
3 tablespoons lemon juice
2 teaspoons chopped fresh parsley
Lemon wedges

Rinse fish thoroughly in cold water; pat dry. Rub fish with salt and pepper; dredge in flour.

Melt ½ cup butter in a large skillet over medium heat. Add fish; sauté 8 minutes on each side or until fish flakes easily when tested with a fork. Transfer fish to a warm serving platter; sprinkle with lemon juice and chopped parsley. Set aside, and keep warm.

Brown remaining butter in a small saucepan; pour over fish. Garnish with lemon wedges, and serve immediately. Yield: 2 to 4 servings.

SHAD

BAKED SHAD

1 (2½-pound) dressed shad
1 teaspoon salt
½ teaspoon pepper
3 tablespoons butter or
  margarine, melted
Lemon slices
Fresh parsley sprigs

Rinse fish thoroughly in cold water; pat dry. Sprinkle fish with salt and pepper; place fish in a well-greased 12- x 8- x 2-inch baking dish. Pour butter over fish.

Bake, uncovered, at 400° for 25 minutes or until fish flakes easily when tested with a fork. Transfer fish to a warm serving platter; garnish with lemon and parsley. Serve immediately. Yield: 6 to 8 servings.

The East Coast English were a long time acquiring a taste for shad. Difficult to eat, shad were also so commonplace as to be thought useful only to the poor. There are stories of families having shad for dinner who, on hearing a knock at the door, would hide their meal before answering. The passive shad was easily caught, which encouraged experimenting. Jefferson had them caught by the barrelful to stock his ponds at Monticello.

Catching shad, Harper's New Monthly Magazine, *1879.*

BAKED SHAD WITH ROE STUFFING

1 (4-pound) dressed shad
1 pair shad roe
4 cups water, divided
2 tablespoons vinegar
½ cup finely chopped onion
½ cup butter or margarine
3 eggs, lightly beaten
1 cup soft breadcrumbs
Salt and pepper to taste
½ cup lemon juice
2 tablespoons Worcestershire
  sauce
Dash of hot sauce
Fresh chopped parsley

Rinse fish thoroughly in cold water; pat dry. Set aside.

Combine roe, 2 cups water, and vinegar in a large saucepan. Bring to a boil; boil 20 minutes. Drain well. Remove and discard membrane. Mash roe in a medium mixing bowl; set aside.

Sauté onion in butter in a small saucepan until tender; stir into mashed roe. Add eggs, breadcrumbs, and salt and pepper, mixing well.

Stuff cavity of fish with roe mixture; secure with metal skewers. Place fish in a 13- x 9- x 2-inch baking pan.

Combine remaining water, lemon juice, Worcestershire sauce, and hot sauce in a mixing bowl; mix well. Pour sauce into pan with fish. Bake, uncovered, at 350° for 35 minutes or until fish flakes easily when tested with a fork, basting often with pan drippings.

Transfer fish to a warm serving platter; garnish with parsley. Serve immediately. Yield: 6 servings.

Bringing up a net full of shad on the Potomac River, c.1900.

PLANKED SHAD

Salt and pepper
1 (4- to 5-pound) dressed
  shad, filleted
¼ cup butter or margarine,
  divided
3 cups mashed, cooked
  potatoes
¼ cup chopped fresh parsley
Lemon slices

Sprinkle salt and pepper on
both sides of each fillet. Place fillets, skin side down, in the center of a wooden plank or large
ovenproof platter; dot with 2 tablespoons butter. Spoon potatoes around edges of fillets.
Broil fish and potatoes 5 to 6
inches from heating element 10
minutes or until fish flakes easily when tested with a fork and
potatoes are lightly browned.
Remove from oven, and dot fish
with remaining butter. Sprinkle
with parsley, and garnish with
lemon slices. Serve immediately. Yield: 6 servings.

BROILED SHAD ROE

1 pair shad roe
2¼ teaspoons salt, divided
2 teaspoons vinegar
⅛ teaspoon pepper
1 tablespoon butter or
  margarine, melted
Chopped fresh parsley

Place roe with water to cover
in a heavy skillet; add 2 teaspoons salt and vinegar. Simmer 15 minutes; remove from
heat, and drain. Immediately
cover with cold water, and let
stand 5 minutes. Drain. Carefully remove loose membrane to
separate roe into 2 portions.
Place roe on rack of broiler
pan. Sprinkle with remaining
salt and pepper; brush with
melted butter. Broil 5 inches
from heating element 5 minutes
on each side or until lightly
browned. Transfer to a warm
serving platter; sprinkle with
parsley, and serve immediately.
Yield: 2 servings.

FRIED SHAD ROE

1 slice bacon
1 pair shad roe
¼ teaspoon salt
⅛ teaspoon pepper
Lemon wedges
Fresh parsley sprigs

Cook bacon in a medium skillet until crisp; drain, reserving 1
tablespoon drippings in skillet.
Crumble bacon; set aside.
Wipe roe gently, using a damp
piece of cheesecloth, being careful not to break membrane.
Place roe in skillet; cover and
cook over low heat 10 minutes.
Remove cover; sprinkle roe with
salt and pepper. Gently turn
roe, being careful not to break
membrane. Cover; cook over low
heat 5 minutes. Uncover, and
cook until lightly browned.
Transfer roe to a warm serving platter. Sprinkle with reserved bacon, and garnish with
lemon and parsley. Serve hot.
Yield: 2 servings.

SNAPPER

GREEK-STYLE BAKED SNAPPER

½ cup olive oil
4 medium onions, chopped
4 cloves garlic, minced
1 cup chopped celery
1 small green pepper, chopped
5 medium tomatoes, peeled and quartered
1 cup water
1 teaspoon dried whole oregano
¼ teaspoon salt
¼ teaspoon pepper
1 (2-pound) dressed snapper
1 tablespoon olive oil
Watercress (optional)

Combine first 10 ingredients in a large skillet. Cook over medium heat 15 minutes or until vegetables are tender.

Rinse fish thoroughly in cold water; pat dry, and place in a greased 13- x 9- x 2-inch baking pan. Brush fish with 1 tablespoon olive oil. Spoon vegetable mixture over fish. Bake, uncovered, at 325° for 45 minutes or until fish flakes easily when tested with a fork.

Transfer fish to a serving platter; spoon vegetables around fish. Garnish with watercress, if desired. Serve immediately. Yield: 2 servings.

BAKED SNAPPER WITH OYSTER SAUCE

1 (4¼-pound) dressed red snapper
1 large onion, sliced
1 bay leaf
1 tablespoon salt, divided
1 large onion, chopped
1 tablespoon butter or margarine
6 mushrooms, thinly sliced
3 large tomatoes, peeled and chopped
1 tablespoon chopped fresh parsley
1 teaspoon dried whole thyme
¼ teaspoon pepper
1 (12-ounce) container Standard oysters, undrained
Fresh parsley sprigs

Rinse fish thoroughly in cold water; pat dry. Place fish in a greased shallow baking pan. Top with sliced onion, bay leaf, and 2 teaspoons salt. Bake, uncovered, at 350° for 1 hour.

Sauté chopped onion in butter in a large skillet until tender. Add mushrooms, tomatoes, chopped parsley, thyme, remaining salt, and pepper. Cook over medium heat until vegetables are tender. Drain oysters, reserving liquid; set oysters aside. Stir oyster liquid into sauce mixture. Cover; simmer 20 minutes. Stir in oysters. Remove from heat.

Pour sauce over fish. Bake, uncovered, at 350° for 30 minutes or until fish flakes easily when tested with a fork.

Transfer fish to a serving platter. Remove and discard bay leaf. Spoon sauce over fish; garnish with parsley sprigs. Yield: 6 servings.

RED SNAPPER FLORIDIAN

½ cup chopped onion
3 tablespoons vegetable oil
2 teaspoons grated orange rind
3 tablespoons orange juice
1 teaspoon salt
4 red snapper fillets (about 2½ pounds)
Ground nutmeg
Pepper
Orange slices
Mint leaves

Combine first 5 ingredients in a 13- x 9- x 2-inch baking dish. Place fillets in dish, turning to coat well. Cover and let stand, skin side up, at least 30 minutes at room temperature.

Turn fish, skin side down, in baking dish. Sprinkle with nutmeg and pepper. Bake, uncovered, at 400° for 25 minutes or until fish flakes easily when tested with a fork, basting occasionally with pan juices.

Transfer fillets to a serving platter. Garnish with orange slices and mint leaves. Serve immediately. Yield: 4 servings.

Red Snapper Floridian combines two of that state's outstanding products for a luscious dish that's ready in minutes.

POACHED RED SNAPPER IN ASPIC

1 (5-pound) whole-dressed red
  snapper, fins and eyes
  removed
3 quarts water
1 quart Chablis or other dry
  white wine, divided
3 envelopes unflavored
  gelatin
¼ teaspoon red food coloring
1 radish
Endive
Watercress
Cherry tomatoes
Zucchini strips
Cucumber slices
Broccoli flowerettes
Caviar Dip

Rinse fish thoroughly in cold water. Place on rack in a fish poacher or tie fish in cheesecloth, and place in a large shallow roasting pan. Add water and 3 cups wine. Place poacher over 2 surface units; cover with lid. Cook over medium heat 20 minutes or until water starts to "quiver." (Do not boil.) Reduce heat to low; cover and cook 40 minutes. (Do not let water boil.)

Transfer fish to a large platter; remove cheesecloth, if used. Cool; refrigerate until chilled.

Soften gelatin in remaining wine in a small saucepan. Stir in food coloring. Cook mixture over low heat, stirring constantly, until gelatin dissolves. Remove from heat.

Place strips of waxed paper under outside edges of fish. Place radish in eye cavity. Using a soft-bristled paint or pastry brush, paint liquid gelatin mixture over surface of fish; repeat procedure until all gelatin mixture is used. Carefully remove waxed paper. Chill thoroughly.

Garnish platter with endive, watercress, cherry tomatoes, zucchini strips, cucumber slices, and broccoli flowerettes. Before serving, peel off aspic and skin, leaving white fish exposed to serve. Serve cold with Caviar Dip. Yield: 15 to 20 appetizer servings.

Caviar Dip:

1 cup mayonnaise
1 (8-ounce) carton
  commercial sour cream
2 tablespoons minced onion
2 hard-cooked eggs, finely
  chopped
Juice of 1 lime
1 clove garlic, minced
¼ teaspoon white pepper
5 tablespoons caviar

Combine first 7 ingredients in a medium mixing bowl; stir well. Chill thoroughly. Stir in caviar immediately before serving. Yield: 2½ cups.

Note: Dip may also be served with raw vegetables or crackers.

The early 1900s were the heyday of postcards, funny and sentimental. In 1910, this card from Fort Myers promised a "big" catch.

It Takes a Ford to Bring a Single One Home.

GREETINGS FROM FORT MYERS, FLA.

STRIPED BASS

BAKED STRIPED BASS

2½ pounds striped bass
  fillets, cut into serving-size
  pieces
1 teaspoon salt, divided
¼ teaspoon pepper, divided
2 large tomatoes, peeled
  and sliced
1 large onion, sliced
3 tablespoons vegetable
  oil
2 tablespoons chopped
  fresh parsley

Place fillets in a 13- x 9- x 2-inch baking dish; sprinkle with ½ teaspoon salt and ⅛ teaspoon pepper. Arrange tomato and onion slices over fish; sprinkle with remaining salt and pepper. Drizzle oil over vegetables.

Bake, uncovered, at 350° for 20 minutes or until fish flakes easily when tested with a fork. Sprinkle with parsley, and serve immediately. Yield: 6 servings.

Striped "Basse" were so plentiful off the Virginia coast, as Captain Smith observed, one might ". . . go over their backs drishod." At the turn of this century some striped bass, incorrectly called rockfish, weighed up to 100 pounds. Size and numbers have dwindled since the days when colonists ate only the heads and used the rest for salting or fertilizers.

Baked Striped Bass: Good idea!

GRILLED STRIPED BASS

6 (¾-inch-thick) striped bass
  steaks (about 2 pounds)
½ cup butter or margarine,
  melted
⅓ cup sherry
⅓ cup lemon juice
3 tablespoons soy sauce
2 tablespoons dried dillweed,
  crushed
1 clove garlic, minced
1 teaspoon salt
2 tablespoons butter, melted
Fresh parsley sprigs
Lemon slices

Rinse steaks thoroughly in cold water; pat dry, and place in a 13- x 9- x 2-inch baking dish.

Combine ½ cup butter, sherry, lemon juice, soy sauce, dillweed, garlic, and salt in a small bowl; stir well, and pour over steaks. Cover; marinate at room temperature 30 minutes, turning steaks once.

Remove steaks from marinade; reserve marinade. Grill steaks 4 inches from hot coals 10 minutes on each side or until fish flakes easily when tested with a fork, basting frequently with reserved marinade.

Transfer steaks to a warm serving platter, and pour 2 tablespoons melted butter over fish. Garnish with parsley and lemon. Yield: 6 servings.

STRIPED BASS BAKE

1 (2-pound) dressed striped
  bass
2 teaspoons salt, divided
¼ teaspoon pepper
3 slices bacon
4 medium potatoes, peeled
  and sliced
2 medium onions, sliced
2 cups water
1 (8-ounce) can tomato sauce
Lemon wedges
Fresh parsley sprigs

Rinse fish thoroughly in cold water; pat dry. Rub fish inside and out with 1 teaspoon salt and pepper. Cut 3 slits in top side of fish; stuff each opening with 1 slice bacon. Set aside.

Place potatoes, onion, and remaining salt in a small Dutch oven. Add water; cover and steam until tender. Drain vegetables, reserving ½ cup cooking liquid; set vegetables aside, and keep liquid warm.

Place fish in a well-greased 13- x 9- x 2-inch baking dish. Bake, uncovered, at 400° for 10 minutes or until fish is lightly browned. Remove fish from oven; arrange potatoes and onions over top. Pour tomato sauce and reserved liquid over vegetables. Return to 400° oven, and bake 20 minutes or until fish flakes easily when tested with a fork, basting once with pan drippings.

Garnish with lemon wedges and parsley sprigs; serve immediately. Yield: 4 to 6 servings.

A big day for these two Mayport, Florida, men in November, 1900. Twelve (count them) bass.

SWORDFISH

PEPPERED SWORDFISH STEAKS

4 (1-inch-thick) swordfish
  steaks
½ cup Chablis or other dry
  white wine
¼ cup lemon juice
2 tablespoons soy sauce
1 tablespoon Worcestershire
  sauce
2 medium cloves garlic,
  minced
Cracked black pepper
Fresh watercress (optional)
Tangy Mustard Sauce

Rinse steaks thoroughly with
cold water; drain and pat dry.
Place steaks in a large shallow
container. Combine white wine,
lemon juice, soy sauce, Worcestershire sauce, and garlic; pour
over steaks. Cover and marinate
at least 4 hours, turning steaks
twice.

Remove steaks from mari-
nade; discard marinade. Lightly
coat one side of each steak with
pepper. Place steaks in a wire
grilling basket. Grill over medium coals 18 minutes on each
side or until fish flakes easily
when tested with a fork.

Transfer steaks to a serving
platter; garnish with watercress, if desired. Serve immediately with Tangy Mustard
Sauce. Yield: 4 servings.

*Peppered Swordfish Steaks
cooked to perfection after
marinating. Tangy Mustard
Sauce adds piquancy.
Too much pepper? No,
cooking cools it.*

Tangy Mustard Sauce:

1½ cups half-and-half, divided
⅓ cup sugar
3 tablespoons dry mustard
1 tablespoon all-purpose flour
½ teaspoon salt
3 egg yolks
⅓ cup vinegar

Pour 1 cup half-and-half into
a small saucepan; cook over low
heat, stirring occasionally, until
bubbly. Combine next 5 ingredients with remaining half-and-
half, mixing well; gradually add
to heated half-and-half, mix
well. Cook over low heat, stirring constantly, until thickened
and smooth.

Remove sauce from heat, and
gradually stir in vinegar. Serve
hot. Yield: 2 cups.

GRILLED SWORDFISH

6 (1-inch-thick) swordfish
  steaks (about 2 pounds)
½ cup vegetable oil
¼ cup lemon juice
2 teaspoons salt
¼ teaspoon white pepper
½ teaspoon Worcestershire
  sauce
Dash of hot sauce
Paprika
Lemon wedges (optional)

Rinse steaks thoroughly in cold water; pat dry. Cut fish into 6 serving-size pieces, and place in a well-greased wire grilling basket. Set aside.

Combine next 6 ingredients. Baste fish with lemon juice mixture; sprinkle with paprika.

Grill over medium coals 8 minutes on each side or until fish flakes easily when tested with a fork, basting frequently with lemon juice mixture and sprinkling with paprika. Serve with lemon wedges, if desired. Yield: 6 servings.

SWORDFISH SUPREME

½ pound fresh mushrooms,
  sliced
1 medium-size green pepper,
  sliced into rings
1 medium onion, sliced and
  separated into rings
½ cup olive oil
1 pound swordfish fillets,
  cubed
¼ teaspoon salt
¼ teaspoon ground oregano
¼ teaspoon paprika
⅛ teaspoon pepper
1 (2-ounce) can flat
  anchovies, drained
Hot cooked rice

Sauté mushrooms, green pepper, and onion in olive oil in a large skillet. Add fillet cubes; brown on all sides over medium heat. Stir in seasonings. Add anchovies; cover and steam 10 minutes or until fish flakes easily when tested with a fork. Serve immediately over rice. Yield: 4 servings.

MARINATED SWORDFISH STEAKS

1½ cups butter or margarine
¾ cup lemon juice
½ cup soy sauce
3 tablespoons Dijon mustard
3 tablespoons dill pickle
  juice
3 tablespoons liquid crab and
  shrimp boil
3 tablespoons garlic powder
6 (1½-inch-thick) swordfish
  steaks (about 3 pounds)
Lemon slices

Melt butter in a medium saucepan. Add lemon juice, soy sauce, mustard, dill sauce, crab and shrimp boil, and garlic powder; mix well. Cook mixture over medium heat, stirring occasionally, until thoroughly heated. Remove from heat; cool.

Rinse steaks thoroughly in cold water, and pat dry. Place steaks in a large shallow container; pour prepared marinade over steaks. Cover and refrigerate 4 to 6 hours, turning steaks occasionally.

Remove steaks from marinade, reserving marinade. Grill over hot coals 18 minutes on each side or until fish flakes easily when tested with a fork, basting frequently with reserved marinade. Transfer steaks to a warm serving platter; serve immediately with lemon slices. Yield: 6 servings.

D istributed throughout the world's warmer oceans, the swordfish has firm, flavorful meat. Most of us purchase it in the form of frozen steaks, but it is available in some Southern markets during summer and fall. Mako shark meat is sometimes substituted for swordfish, but shark is noticeably darker. Since swordfish tends toward dryness, it is well to marinate or baste it.

BAKED SWORDFISH STEAKS

1 small onion, thinly sliced
6 (1-inch-thick) swordfish
  steaks (about 2 pounds)
1½ cups chopped fresh
  mushrooms
1 medium tomato, chopped
¼ cup chopped green pepper
¼ cup chopped fresh parsley
3 tablespoons diced pimiento,
  drained
½ cup Chablis or other dry
  white wine
2 tablespoons lemon juice
1 teaspoon salt
¼ teaspoon dried dillweed
⅛ teaspoon pepper
Lime wedges

Line a well-greased 12- x 8- x 2-inch baking dish with onion slices. Rinse steaks thoroughly in cold water, and pat dry. Place steaks on top of onion. Combine remaining vegetables in a medium mixing bowl; spread over top of fish. Combine wine, lemon juice, salt, dillweed, and pepper in a small mixing bowl; pour over vegetables. Bake, uncovered, at 350° for 35 minutes or until fish flakes easily when tested with a fork.

Transfer fish and vegetables to a warm serving platter. Serve immediately with lime wedges. Yield: 6 servings.

*Now that the feisty
swordfish is stilled,
a cautious inspection
is safe. Florida, c.1920.*

TUNA

GRILLED TUNA STEAKS

12 (1-inch-thick) tuna steaks
   (about 6 pounds)
1 cup lemon juice
½ cup soy sauce
2 bay leaves
½ teaspoon dried whole
   thyme

Rinse steaks thoroughly in cold water, and pat dry. Place steaks in a 15- x 10- x 1-inch jellyroll pan.

Combine lemon juice, soy sauce, bay leaves, and thyme, mixing well. Pour mixture over steaks; cover and marinate in refrigerator 1 hour, turning steaks often.

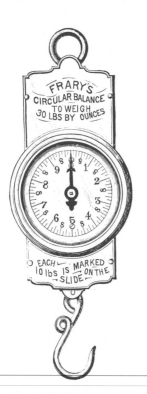

Remove steaks, and place in two well-greased wire grilling baskets; reserve marinade. Grill over hot coals 20 minutes or until steaks flake easily when tested with a fork, turning and basting occasionally with reserved marinade. Serve immediately. Yield: 12 servings.

TUNA STEAKS WITH MUSHROOM SAUCE

4 (¾-inch-thick) tuna steaks
   (about 1½ pounds)
Salt and pepper to taste
1 clove garlic, thinly sliced
2 tablespoons butter or
   margarine
1 tablespoon lemon juice
½ pound fresh mushrooms,
   sliced
1 (10¾-ounce) can chicken
   broth, undiluted
2 tablespoons soy sauce
2 tablespoons cornstarch
Hot cooked rice

Rinse steaks thoroughly in cold water, and sprinkle with salt and pepper; set aside.

Sauté garlic in butter in a large skillet until tender; add lemon juice and steaks to skillet. Cook over medium heat, turning steaks once, until fish flakes easily when tested with a fork. Transfer fish to a warm serving platter. Reserve drippings in skillet.

Sauté mushrooms in skillet until tender. Add chicken broth, soy sauce, and cornstarch. Cook over medium heat, stirring constantly, until sauce thickens.

Spoon sauce over steak. Serve immediately with hot cooked rice. Yield: 4 servings.

CREAMED TUNA

2 tablespoons butter or
   margarine
2 tablespoons all-purpose
   flour
½ teaspoon salt
1 cup milk
1 (6½-ounce) can tuna,
   drained and flaked
Toast points

Melt butter in a medium saucepan over low heat; add flour and salt, stirring until smooth. Cook 1 minute, stirring constantly. Gradually add 1 cup milk; cook over medium heat, stirring constantly, until mixture is thickened and bubbly. Gently fold in flaked tuna, and continue cooking until mixture is thoroughly heated. Serve warm over toast points. Yield: 4 servings.

About 350 B.C. Aristotle constructed a wonderful mythology about tuna that persisted for centuries. As "facts," he stated that the tuna navigated by keeping a sharp eye on the shore and that it alternately sank to the bottom and rose to the top of the water as it slept. We in the South may think of tuna as that can of albacore that comes from the West Coast; let's keep it that way. A 400-pound tuna, beef-red when fresh, needs a professional butcher to cut it into steaks.

TUNA POT PIE

1 cup diced potato
½ cup diced carrot
3 tablespoons chopped green
  pepper
3 tablespoons chopped onion
1 cup water
1½ teaspoons salt, divided
1 (8½-ounce) can green peas,
  drained
2 tablespoons butter or
  margarine
1 cup plus 2 tablespoons
  all-purpose flour, divided
Milk
Dash of pepper
1 (9¼-ounce) can tuna,
  drained and flaked
⅓ cup shortening
2 tablespoons ice water

Combine potato, carrot, green pepper, onion, 1 cup water, and ½ teaspoon salt in a small saucepan. Simmer, uncovered, 15 minutes, stirring occasionally. Stir in peas. Drain vegetables, reserving cooking liquid. Set vegetables and liquid aside.

Melt butter in a large saucepan over low heat; add 2 tablespoons flour, stirring until smooth. Cook 1 minute, stirring constantly. Add milk to reserved cooking liquid to equal 2 cups; gradually add to flour mixture. Cook over medium heat, stirring constantly, until thickened and bubbly. Stir in ½ teaspoon salt and pepper. Gently fold in tuna and reserved vegetables. Pour mixture into a lightly greased 1½-quart casserole, and set aside.

Combine remaining flour and salt in a small mixing bowl. Cut in shortening with a pastry blender until mixture resembles coarse meal. Sprinkle with ice water, and stir with a fork just until all dry ingredients are moistened. Shape into a ball.

Roll pastry out on a lightly floured surface to fit top of casserole. Carefully place pastry over top of dish, crimping edges to seal. Make several slits in pastry to allow steam to escape. Bake at 450° for 20 minutes or until pastry is lightly browned. Remove from oven, and serve hot. Yield: 6 servings.

Tuna Salad, without which life as we know it would be impossible.

TUNA CASSEROLE

¼ cup butter or margarine
¼ cup all-purpose flour
2½ cups milk
1 teaspoon salt
¼ teaspoon pepper
1 (6½-ounce) can tuna,
  drained and flaked
1 cup chopped fresh
  mushrooms
1 cup crushed potato chips

Melt butter in a saucepan over low heat; add flour, stirring until smooth. Cook 1 minute, stirring constantly. Gradually add milk; cook over medium heat, stirring constantly, until thickened and bubbly. Stir in salt and pepper. Fold in tuna and mushrooms.

Spoon tuna mixture into a lightly greased 1-quart casserole; top with potato chips. Bake, uncovered, at 375° for 30 minutes. Serve hot. Yield: 4 servings.

TUNA SALAD

½ cup mayonnaise
¼ cup commercial sour
  cream
1 tablespoon lemon juice
½ teaspoon prepared
  horseradish
1 teaspoon dried whole
  dillweed
3 tablespoons capers, drained
  (optional)
⅛ teaspoon salt
1 small cucumber, peeled and
  cubed (about 1 cup)
2 (6½-ounce) cans tuna,
  drained and flaked
6 medium tomatoes, peeled
Leaf lettuce

Combine mayonnaise, sour cream, lemon juice, horseradish, dillweed, capers, if desired, and salt in a medium mixing bowl, stirring well. Add cucumber and tuna, stirring well. Cover and refrigerate until chilled.

Cut each tomato into 8 wedges, cutting to, but not through, base of tomato. Spread wedges apart to form shell. Spoon tuna salad into tomato shells. Place on a lettuce-lined serving plate. Serve immediately. Yield: 4 to 6 servings.

FRESHWATER REWARDS

On a cool day in spring, a boy with a cane pole sits in a patch of shade on a North Carolina creek bank waiting for a nibble. He hopes the crappie and bluegill are biting; he can almost taste them, done up in cornmeal and crisply fried. The couple encamped by a Georgia river pick a spot where the water moves slowly. They wet their lines, hungry for a mess of catfish. A solitary man in waders enters a trout stream that rushes down a West Virginia hillside: another Southerner re-enacting the ancient ritual of angling for earth's oldest living vertebrate.

Inland fishermen know they are no more likely to pull up a pompano or a flounder than the Gulf shrimper is to find a fiesty rainbow in his nets. That is because an invisible barrier of salt separates the marine life of fresh water ponds, lakes and streams from the oceans and seas. With rare exceptions, a given fish can live only in one or the other.

Looking at the immense popularity of the fish fry in the modern-day South, it is hard to believe statistics that place this country behind China, Russia, and Japan in fish consumption. Our appetite is growing by leaps and bounds, however, and one of the reasons is the development of the fish farming industry, along with a public relations blitz that has brought the image of the catfish to a high gloss.

"Fish Fry Every Friday, 6 p.m.," the signs still say. Held on the grounds or in some spacious basement, the fish fry is a Southern institution. The menu is comfortingly predictable: fish deep-fried after coating in seasoned white (not yellow) cornmeal, coleslaw, hush puppies, sliced white bread, and baked beans or corn-on-the-cob in season. This meal has kept families playing together while separating them from enough money to keep their churches and civic groups in the good works business.

Many fishermen place catfish up there with bass as a sporty catch in the streams, while in the aquaculture industry of the rich Mississippi Delta, catfish has joined cotton as a cash crop. Two cardinal rules apply, whether we are cooking pan-dressed sunfish or fillets or steaks: Use utterly fresh fish and never overcook them!

A dockside feast awaits the deserving fishermen. Country-Fried Catfish with Hush Puppies (page 111) served with coleslaw, tomatoes, and a tall pitcher of iced tea.

BASS

BAKED BASS

1 (4-pound) dressed
  freshwater bass
2 tablespoons vegetable oil
½ teaspoon salt
¼ teaspoon pepper
1 small onion, finely chopped
2 teaspoons Worcestershire
  sauce
¼ cup orange juice
1 tablespoon lemon juice
½ cup water
Lemon slices

Rinse fish thoroughly, and
pat dry. Rub inside and outside
of fish with oil. Sprinkle fish
with salt and pepper; place
onion in cavity.

Place fish in an aluminum
foil-lined 13- x 9- x 2-inch baking pan. Pour Worcestershire
sauce and juices over fish. Add
water to pan.

Bake, uncovered, at 400° for
30 minutes or until fish flakes
easily when tested with a fork.
Baste fish frequently with pan
drippings.

Transfer fish to a warm serving platter. Garnish with lemon
slices. Yield: 4 servings.

BAKED BASS IN WINE

1 (3-pound) dressed
  freshwater bass
¼ cup butter or margarine,
  melted
1 tablespoon all-purpose
  flour
½ teaspoon salt
¼ teaspoon pepper
¼ teaspoon garlic powder
½ cup Chablis or other dry
  white wine
2 limes, cut into wedges

Rinse fish thoroughly, and
pat dry. Make 3 shallow diagonal cuts in both sides of fish.
Brush fish inside and out with
melted butter; dust with flour.
Sprinkle with salt, pepper, and
garlic powder.

Place fish in a well-greased 13-
x 9- x 2-inch baking dish; add
wine to baking dish. Bake, uncovered, at 450° for 30 minutes
or until fish flakes easily when
tested with a fork, basting occasionally with pan drippings.

Transfer fish to a warm serving platter. Garnish with lime
wedges. Yield: 4 servings.

*"Catfish" Smith (right) and
his brother did not
restrict their catch to
"cats," as shown in this
studio photograph taken
in Albany, Georgia, c.1890.*

Georgia Department of Archives and History

BAKED BASS WITH BACON

6 (½-pound) dressed
   freshwater bass
½ cup cornmeal
1½ teaspoons salt
1½ teaspoons paprika
6 slices bacon
3 tomatoes, peeled and each
   cut into 6 wedges

Rinse fish in cold water, and pat dry.

Combine cornmeal, salt, and paprika in a medium mixing bowl; dredge fish in cornmeal mixture. Place fish in a greased 13- x 9- x 2-inch baking pan. Place bacon on top of fish.

Bake, uncovered, at 425° for 20 minutes. Remove from oven; place tomatoes around fish. Broil 5 inches from heating element 4 minutes or until tomatoes are tender. Serve immediately. Yield: 6 servings.

BASS BAKE

8 freshwater bass fillets
   (about 1⅔ pounds)
1 cup soft breadcrumbs
¼ cup butter or margarine
1 tablespoon vinegar
1 tablespoon lemon juice
1 tablespoon Worcestershire
   sauce
1 teaspoon prepared mustard
1 teaspoon salt
⅛ teaspoon pepper
Paprika
Fresh parsley sprigs (optional)

Rinse fish thoroughly; pat dry, and set aside.

Sprinkle breadcrumbs in bottom of a 9-inch square baking pan. Arrange fish over breadcrumbs.

Combine next 7 ingredients in a small saucepan; bring to a boil, stirring until butter melts. Remove from heat; pour over fish. Sprinkle with paprika.

Bake, uncovered, at 450° for 20 minutes or until fish flakes easily when tested with a fork.

Transfer fish to a warm serving platter. Garnish with parsley, if desired. Yield: 4 servings.

Wilmington Island Baked Bass contains a savory stuffing.

WILMINGTON ISLAND BAKED BASS

1 (2-pound) dressed
   freshwater bass
¼ cup all-purpose flour
¼ cup butter or margarine,
   melted
2 tablespoons half-and-half
2 cups soft breadcrumbs
½ cup peeled, seeded,
   chopped tomato
½ cup chopped onion
¼ cup peeled, seeded,
   chopped cucumber
¼ cup chopped celery
3 tablespoons butter or
   margarine, melted
1 tablespoon chopped
   celery leaves
½ teaspoon salt
¼ teaspoon pepper
1½ cups milk

Rinse fish thoroughly; pat dry, and set aside.

Combine flour, ¼ cup butter, and half-and-half, mixing well. Set aside.

Combine breadcrumbs, tomato, onion, cucumber, celery, 3 tablespoons melted butter, and chopped celery leaves in a large mixing bowl; stir mixture well. Sprinkle fish cavity evenly with salt and pepper, and place stuffing in cavity. Close opening with wooden picks, and tie with string.

Place prepared fish in a large shallow roasting pan, and spread flour mixture evenly over top. Pour 1½ cups milk around fish. Bake, uncovered, at 400° for 45 minutes or until fish flakes easily when tested with a fork, basting occasionally with pan drippings.

Transfer fish to a warm serving platter. Serve immediately. Yield: about 4 servings.

Franklin D. Roosevelt enjoying his favorite sport at his favorite place, Warm Springs, Georgia, 1930.

Franklin Roosevelt Library

BAKED BASS FILLETS

6 freshwater bass fillets
   (about 2 pounds)
¾ cup white wine
¼ cup lemon juice
1 chicken-flavored bouillon
   cube, crushed
1 clove garlic, minced
2 tablespoons butter or
   margarine, melted
3 eggs, beaten
½ cup all-purpose flour
Chopped fresh parsley
Paprika

Rinse fish thoroughly in cold water; pat dry, and set aside.

Combine wine, lemon juice, bouillon cube, and garlic in a small mixing bowl; mix well, and set aside.

Pour melted butter into a 13- x 9- x 2-inch baking dish. Dip fish in egg, and dredge in flour. Place fish in prepared dish. Bake, uncovered, at 350° for 10 minutes. Pour reserved wine mixture over top, and bake an additional 10 minutes or until fish flakes easily when tested with a fork.

Sprinkle fish with parsley and paprika. Serve immediately. Yield: 6 servings.

BROILED BLACK BASS

4 (¾-pound) dressed
   freshwater bass
1 tablespoon butter or
   margarine, melted
¾ teaspoon salt, divided
¼ teaspoon pepper
2 tablespoons butter or
   margarine, melted
⅛ teaspoon red pepper
1 tablespoon chopped fresh
   parsley
2 tablespoons lemon juice
Fresh parsley sprigs
Lemon slices

Rinse fish thoroughly; pat dry. Combine 1 tablespoon butter, ½ teaspoon salt, and ¼ teaspoon pepper; rub over fish.

Arrange fish on rack in a shallow roasting pan; broil 4 inches from heating element 5 minutes. Turn fish, and broil 5 minutes or until fish flakes easily when tested with a fork.

Remove fish to a serving platter; brush with 2 tablespoons butter. Season with remaining salt, red pepper, chopped parsley, and lemon juice. Garnish with parsley and lemon. Serve warm. Yield: 4 servings.

PAN-FRIED BASS

4 (¾-pound) dressed
   freshwater bass
1 teaspoon salt
½ teaspoon pepper
½ cup all-purpose flour
½ cup cornmeal
¼ cup butter or margarine
¼ cup bacon drippings
Chopped fresh parsley
Lemon wedges

Rinse fish thoroughly in cold water; pat dry. Make a shallow S-shaped cut on each side. Sprinkle fish with salt and pepper; set aside.

Combine flour and cornmeal; stir well. Dredge fish in flour mixture.

Heat butter and bacon drippings in a large skillet to 350°. Cook fish 15 minutes on each side or until golden brown. Drain well on paper towels.

Transfer fish to a warm serving platter; sprinkle with parsley, and garnish with lemon wedges. Serve immediately. Yield: 4 servings.

DEEP-FRIED BASS

4 pounds freshwater bass
  fillets
1 tablespoon salt
1 cup yellow cornmeal
Peanut oil
Lemon wedges
Fresh parsley sprigs

Rinse fish thoroughly in cold water; pat dry. Sprinkle fish with salt.

Dredge fish in cornmeal, shaking off any excess cornmeal. Carefully drop fish into deep hot oil (375°). Fry 3 minutes or until fish is golden brown; drain well on paper towels.

Transfer fish to a warm serving platter, and garnish with lemon wedges and parsley sprigs. Serve immediately. Yield: 12 servings.

Black Bass Spearing.
Currier and Ives, c.1800.

N aturalist William Bartram, on his 1765 trek through the South, found the Florida Seminoles fishing for largemouth bass. They used braided deer hair for line, as the Europeans had been using horsehair. But the typical American Indian did not fish for bass; largemouths and smallmouths alike are fighting fish, more suitable to the relaxed sport fisherman than to a hungry man in a hurry. When cooking, opt for the smaller sizes for best flavor, as in our Pine Bark Stew. Members of the Otranto Club of South Carolina explain that the name derives from the fact that it was cooked over a fire of pine bark.

BARBECUED BASS

8 freshwater bass fillets
  (about 2½ pounds)
1 teaspoon salt
¼ teaspoon pepper
¼ teaspoon paprika
8 slices bacon
1 tablespoon plus 1 teaspoon
  lemon juice, divided

Rinse fish thoroughly in cold water; pat dry. Sprinkle fish with salt, pepper, and paprika; set aside.

Place two bacon slices lengthwise on a 30-inch length of aluminum foil; place a fillet on each slice. Pour 1 teaspoon lemon juice over fillets. Fold foil around fillets, sealing tightly to form a packet. Repeat procedure, making 3 additional packets.

Place packets on grill over hot coals; grill 10 minutes. Turn packets over; grill an additional 10 minutes. Remove from heat; serve on individual dinner plates. Yield: 4 servings.

Orange Steamed Black Bass is prepared in the oriental manner, reminding us how varied our heritage is.

ORANGE STEAMED BLACK BASS

8 freshwater bass fillets
  (about 2 pounds)
⅓ cup orange juice
1 (11-ounce) can mandarin
  oranges, undrained
2 tablespoons soy sauce
2 tablespoons sherry
1 tablespoon peanut oil
½ teaspoon ground ginger
1 bunch green onion tops, cut
  into 2-inch lengths
Hot cooked rice

Rinse fish in cold water; pat dry. Cut fish crosswise into ¾-inch-thick slices. Arrange slices in a 10-inch pieplate. Pour orange juice over fish.

Drain juice from mandarin oranges into a small bowl, reserving fruit. Add soy sauce, sherry, oil, and ginger to mandarin orange juice; stir well. Pour juice mixture over fish. Arrange green onion tops over fish.

Place pieplate on rack in a steamer filled with water to within 1 inch of the top of rack. Bring to a boil; cover steamer. Reduce heat; simmer 12 minutes or until fish flakes easily when tested with a fork.

Remove pieplate from steamer; arrange mandarin orange sections on top of fish. Serve immediately over hot cooked rice. Yield: 6 servings.

OTRANTO PINE BARK STEW

3 pounds freshwater bass
  fillets, cut into serving-size
  pieces
½ pound sliced bacon
4 large baking potatoes,
  peeled and sliced
4 large onions, sliced
1 teaspoon salt
2 cups boiling water, divided
1 tablespoon curry powder,
  divided
Spicy Sauce
Hot cooked rice

Rinse fish thoroughly; pat dry, and set aside.

Cook bacon in a large Dutch oven until crisp. Drain bacon well on paper towels, reserving drippings in Dutch oven. Set bacon aside.

Place one-third of potato slices in bottom of Dutch oven; arrange one-third of onion slices over top. Dissolve salt in 1 cup boiling water, and pour over vegetables in Dutch oven. Cook, uncovered, over medium-low heat 10 minutes.

Arrange one-third of fish over vegetables; sprinkle with 1 teaspoon curry powder. Add a second layer of potatoes, onion, and fish. Pour remaining boiling water over top. Sprinkle with 1 teaspoon curry powder. Layer remaining potatoes, onion, and fish over top. Sprinkle with remaining 1 teaspoon curry powder.

Cover and simmer over medium-low heat 1 hour and 15 minutes or until vegetables are tender and fish flakes easily when tested with a fork.

Drain cooking liquid from stew, reserving 2 cups for use in Spicy Sauce. Prepare Spicy Sauce, and pour over stew. Spoon stew over hot cooked rice, and garnish with reserved bacon slices. Serve immediately. Yield: 8 servings.

Spicy Sauce:

2 cups reserved stew liquid
1 (14-ounce) bottle catsup
½ cup Worcestershire sauce
½ cup butter or margarine,
  melted
1 teaspoon curry powder
¼ teaspoon red pepper
¼ teaspoon black pepper

Combine all ingredients in a large heavy saucepan. Place over medium heat; simmer, stirring frequently, until well blended and thoroughly heated. Serve hot. Yield: about 4 cups.

CATFISH

BROILED CATFISH

4 (¾-pound) dressed catfish, butterflied
½ cup butter
2 tablespoons chopped fresh parsley
2 tablespoons all-purpose flour
1 teaspoon salt
¼ teaspoon pepper
Lemon slices
Fresh parsley sprigs (optional)

Rinse fish thoroughly in cold water; pat dry, and set aside.

Melt butter in a small saucepan; stir in chopped parsley, and set aside.

Combine flour, salt, and pepper; dredge fish in flour mixture. Place fish on rack in a shallow broiling pan. Spoon half of butter mixture over fish.

Broil 4 inches from heating element 5 minutes. Remove from heat; using a spatula, carefully turn fish. Baste with remaining butter mixture; continue broiling an additional 5 minutes or until fish flakes easily when tested with a fork.

Serve immediately with lemon slices. Garnish with parsley, if desired. Yield: 4 servings.

C aptain Smith of Virginia saw fishing for "brookies" and other freshwater fish as pastime as well as food gathering, but angling for fun was not truly smiled upon in the South until the early 1800s when labor became less intense.

ZIPPY BROILED CATFISH

6 dressed catfish (about 4 pounds)
3 tablespoons lemon juice
2 teaspoons salt
¼ teaspoon pepper
1 cup all-purpose flour
1 (8-ounce) bottle commercial Italian dressing
Lemon wedges
Fresh parsley sprigs

Rinse fish thoroughly; pat dry. Brush inside of fish with lemon juice. Sprinkle salt and pepper over fish; dredge in flour. Shake off excess flour.

Place fish on well-greased rack of a shallow broiling pan. Baste fish with half of salad dressing. Broil 4 inches from heating element 6 minutes. Remove from heat; using a spatula, carefully turn fish. Baste with remaining salad dressing. Continue broiling an additional 5 minutes or until fish flakes easily when tested with a fork.

Transfer to a warm serving platter. Garnish with lemon wedges and parsley. Serve immediately. Yield: 6 servings.

A Georgia boy and his dog wait for the catfish to bite.

Georgia Department of Archives and History

Roadside stand near Birmingham, photographed by Walker Evans, 1936.

ALABAMA PAN-FRIED CATFISH

6 dressed catfish (about 4
 pounds)
2 teaspoons salt
¼ teaspoon pepper
2 eggs, beaten
2 tablespoons milk
2 cups cornmeal
Vegetable oil
Tartar sauce (page 126)

Rinse fish thoroughly in cold water, and pat dry. Sprinkle fish evenly with salt and pepper, and set aside.

Combine eggs and milk in a medium mixing bowl; mix well. Dip fish in egg mixture, and roll in cornmeal.

Heat ⅛ inch oil to 350° in a large heavy skillet. Add fish, and fry 5 minutes on each side or until golden brown. Drain fish well on paper towels.

Transfer fish to a warm serving platter, and serve immediately with tartar sauce. Yield: 6 servings.

DAPHNE LODGE FRIED CATFISH AND HUSH PUPPIES

4 (¾-pound) dressed catfish
2 cups cornmeal
1 teaspoon salt
2 cups buttermilk
Vegetable oil
Lemon wedges
Tartar sauce (page 126)
Hush Puppies

Rinse fish thoroughly in cold water, and pat dry.

Combine cornmeal and salt. Dip fish in buttermilk, and dredge in cornmeal mixture.

Carefully drop fish into deep hot oil (350°). Fry until fish float to the top and are golden brown; drain well on paper towels. Reserve hot oil for frying Hush Puppies.

Transfer fish to a warm serving platter, and garnish with lemon wedges. Serve immediately with tartar sauce and Hush Puppies. Yield: 4 servings.

Hush Puppies:

½ cup cornmeal
½ cup all-purpose flour
1 teaspoon baking powder
½ teaspoon sugar
¼ teaspoon salt
Pinch of baking soda
½ cup buttermilk
1 egg, lightly beaten
1 small onion, finely chopped
1½ teaspoons vegetable oil
Reserved vegetable oil

Combine cornmeal, flour, baking powder, sugar, and salt in a medium mixing bowl; mix well, and set aside.

Dissolve soda in buttermilk in a small mixing bowl. Add egg, onion, and 1½ teaspoons oil; stir well. Add to dry ingredients, mixing well.

Drop batter by tablespoonfuls into deep, hot oil (350°), cooking only a few at a time. Fry 3 minutes; turn and fry an additional 3 minutes or until hush puppies are golden brown. Drain well on paper towels. Serve immediately. Yield: 1 dozen.

COUNTRY-FRIED CATFISH WITH HUSH PUPPIES

12 (¾-pound) dressed catfish
2 cups all-purpose flour
2 cups fine, dry breadcrumbs
3 eggs, lightly beaten
¼ cup plus 2 tablespoons milk
2¼ teaspoons salt
½ teaspoon pepper
Vegetable oil
Green onion fans (optional)
Tartar sauce (page 126)
Hush Puppies

Rinse fish thoroughly in cold water; pat dry, and set aside.

Combine flour and breadcrumbs in a large mixing bowl; set aside. Combine eggs, milk, salt, and pepper, mixing well. Dip fish in egg mixture, and dredge in flour mixture.

Carefully drop fish into deep hot oil (375°). Fry 12 minutes or until fish float to the top and are golden brown. Drain. Reserve oil for frying Hush Puppies.

Transfer fish to a serving platter; garnish with green onion fans, if desired. Serve hot with tartar sauce and Hush Puppies. Yield: 12 servings.

Hush Puppies:

1⅔ cups cornmeal
¾ cup all-purpose flour
1 tablespoon baking powder
1 teaspoon salt
½ teaspoon pepper
⅓ cup chopped onion
¾ cup milk
¼ cup vegetable oil
2 eggs, lightly beaten
Reserved vegetable oil

Combine cornmeal, flour, baking powder, salt, pepper, and onion in a medium mixing bowl; add milk, ¼ cup vegetable oil, and eggs, stirring well.

Carefully drop batter by tablespoonfuls into deep hot oil (375°), cooking only a few at a time. Fry 3 minutes or until hush puppies are golden brown. Drain well on paper towels. Serve immediately. Yield: about 2 dozen.

FRIED CATFISH SANDWICHES

4 (¾-pound) dressed catfish, butterflied
2 teaspoons salt, divided
2 eggs, beaten
2 tablespoons milk
1 cup white cornmeal
Vegetable oil
4 sandwich rolls
Leaf lettuce
Tartar sauce (page 126)
Catsup (optional)

Rinse fish thoroughly in cold water; pat dry. Sprinkle each fish with ½ teaspoon salt. Place seasoned fish in a covered dish; chill overnight.

Combine eggs and milk; mix well. Dip seasoned fish in egg mixture; coat with cornmeal. Fry in deep hot oil (375°) until golden brown. Drain well on paper towels.

Arrange lettuce on bottom half of each roll; top with fish and tartar sauce. Cover with remaining roll half. Catsup may be added, if desired. Yield: 4 servings.

GRILLED SESAME CATFISH

6 dressed catfish (about 4 pounds)
½ cup vegetable oil
½ cup sesame seeds
¼ cup lemon juice
1 teaspoon salt
Dash of pepper

Rinse fish thoroughly in cold water; pat dry, and set aside.

Combine oil, sesame seeds, lemon juice, salt, and pepper in a small mixing bowl.

Place fish on a well-greased grill 4 inches from medium coals. Cook 12 minutes on each side or until fish flakes easily when tested with a fork. Baste often with sauce. Transfer to a serving platter, and serve immediately. Yield: 6 servings.

Note: Catfish may be placed in a well-greased hinged fish basket and placed on grill.

Fried Catfish Sandwiches, nestled in a napkin-lined basket, are a delightful menu idea for a summer meal.

SMOKED CATFISH

4 (¾-pound) dressed catfish
Salt
Hickory chips, soaked

Rinse fish thoroughly in cold water; pat dry. Coat fish heavily with salt inside and out. Cover and chill overnight.

Rinse salt off fish; pat dry.

Prepare charcoal fire in smoker, and let burn 10 to 15 minutes. Add hickory chips. Place water pan in smoker, and fill with hot water.

Place fish on food rack. Cover smoker with lid; cook 4 hours according to manufacturer's instructions or until fish flakes easily when tested with a fork.

Leave fish in smoker until fire dies down and fish is cool. Transfer fish to a serving platter. Yield: 4 servings.

Note: Smoked catfish may be refrigerated up to 2 weeks.

CATFISH DINNER

4 dressed catfish (about 2¾ pounds), filleted
1 teaspoon salt
½ teaspoon pepper
2 tablespoons Worcestershire sauce
1 small onion, chopped
2 medium potatoes, parboiled, peeled, and thinly sliced
¼ cup butter or margarine
Lemon slices

Rinse fish thoroughly in cold water; pat dry. Place fish in a 13- x 9- x 2-inch baking dish. Sprinkle with salt, pepper, and Worcestershire sauce. Arrange onion and potatoes over top; dot with butter.

Cover and bake at 350° for 45 minutes or until fish flakes easily when tested with a fork. Garnish with lemon slices; serve hot. Yield: 4 servings.

CATFISH STEW

3 slices bacon
1 cup chopped onion
1¼ pounds catfish fillets, divided
1 (28-ounce) can whole tomatoes, undrained
2 cups peeled, diced potatoes
1 cup water
1 tablespoon Worcestershire sauce
1 teaspoon salt
Dash of pepper
⅛ teaspoon ground thyme
⅛ teaspoon hot sauce

Cook bacon in a large Dutch oven until crisp and browned; drain on paper towels. Crumble and set aside, reserving drippings in pan.

Sauté onion in bacon drippings until tender.

Cut ¼ pound fish into ½-inch squares, and add to sautéed onion. Stir in tomatoes, potatoes, water, Worcestershire sauce, salt, pepper, thyme, and hot sauce. Bring mixture to a boil. Reduce heat; cover and simmer 30 minutes.

Cut remaining fish into 1½-inch pieces. Add to stew mixture. Bring to a boil. Reduce heat; cover and simmer 10 minutes or until fish flakes easily when tested with a fork. Stir in reserved bacon. Spoon into serving bowls, and serve immediately. Yield: 2 quarts.

CATFISH ÉTOUFFÉE

2 cloves fresh garlic, minced
1 cup chopped fresh parsley
1 large green pepper, chopped
3 stalks celery, chopped
1 bunch green onions, chopped
5 pounds dressed catfish, filleted and cut into chunks
1 teaspoon salt
1 teaspoon pepper
¼ teaspoon red pepper
3 tablespoons vegetable oil
2 tablespoons all-purpose flour, divided
1 (15-ounce) can tomato sauce, divided
¼ teaspoon ground thyme
1 large bay leaf
2 lemon slices
¼ cup water

Combine garlic, parsley, green pepper, celery, and onion in a medium mixing bowl; mix well, and set aside.

Place fish in a large mixing bowl; sprinkle with salt and pepper. Set aside.

Pour oil into a large Dutch oven; add half of seasoned fish. Sprinkle half of prepared vegetables on top; add 1 tablespoon flour and half of tomato sauce. Do not stir. Repeat layers with remaining fish, vegetables, flour, and tomato sauce. Add thyme, bay leaf, lemon slices, and water. Do not stir.

Cook, uncovered, over medium heat 1 hour or until fish flakes easily when tested with a fork. Shake pot occasionally to prevent sticking. (Do not stir mixture.)

Remove bay leaf; discard. Serve hot in individual serving bowls. Yield: about 2½ quarts.

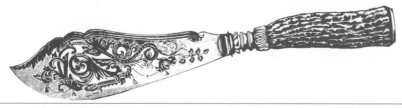

CATFISH IN MUSHROOM CREAM SAUCE

8 catfish fillets (about 1½ pounds)
2 medium carrots, scraped, thinly sliced, and parboiled
¼ cup grated onion
2 tablespoons lemon juice
1 small bay leaf
1 clove garlic, crushed
1 teaspoon dried parsley flakes
¼ teaspoon salt
¼ teaspoon white pepper
¼ cup butter or margarine
Mushroom Cream Sauce
Lemon slices
Fresh parsley sprigs

Rinse fish thoroughly in cold water; pat dry.

Place fish in a greased 13- x 9- x 2-inch baking dish; add water to cover. Add next 8 ingredients, and dot with ¼ cup butter.

Cover and bake at 350° for 25 minutes or until fish flakes easily when tested with a fork.

Drain fish and vegetables; reserve pan liquid for Mushroom Cream Sauce. Remove and discard bay leaf.

Prepare Mushroom Cream Sauce, and pour over fish and vegetables in baking dish; broil 4 inches from heating element 5 minutes or until lightly browned on top. Garnish with lemon slices and fresh parsley sprigs. Serve immediately. Yield: 4 to 6 servings.

Mushroom Cream Sauce:

Reserved pan liquid
¼ cup plus 2 tablespoons butter or margarine, divided
3 tablespoons all-purpose flour
¼ teaspoon salt
¼ teaspoon red pepper
¼ cup milk
¼ cup whipping cream
1 cup sliced fresh mushrooms
⅛ teaspoon pepper
1 teaspoon lemon juice

Place reserved pan liquid in a medium saucepan; bring to a boil. Cook until liquid is reduced to 1 cup; set aside.

Melt ¼ cup butter in a medium saucepan; stir in flour, salt, and red pepper. Add pan liquid. Cook over medium heat until sauce thickens. Add milk and whipping cream, stirring well. Continue cooking over medium heat until mixture begins to boil. Reduce heat, and simmer 2 to 3 minutes, stirring occasionally. Set aside.

Melt remaining butter in a small skillet; add mushrooms, ⅛ teaspoon pepper, and lemon juice. Sauté 5 minutes; drain. Add mushrooms to prepared white sauce, mixing well. Yield: about 2½ cups.

Catfish Étouffée (front) and Catfish in Mushroom Cream Sauce.

CREOLE FRIED CRAPPIE

12 pan-dressed crappie (about 4 pounds)
¼ cup Worcestershire sauce
1 tablespoon salt
1½ teaspoons pepper
½ teaspoon red pepper
¼ teaspoon hot sauce
1 (5¼-ounce) jar Creole mustard
3 cups yellow cornmeal
Vegetable oil

Rinse fish thoroughly in cold water; pat dry, and set aside.

Combine Worcestershire sauce, salt, pepper, and hot sauce; sprinkle over fish. Brush fish on both sides with mustard. Roll in cornmeal.

Fry in deep hot oil (375°) until fish float to the top and are golden brown. Drain well. Transfer to a serving platter, and serve immediately. Yield: 6 servings.

C. M. Henderson & Co. used a toddler in a creel for this 1890s trade card for boots and shoes.

SKILLET CRAPPIE

2½ pounds pan-dressed crappie
¼ cup shortening
2 medium potatoes, peeled and diced
½ cup finely chopped green pepper
1 (14½-ounce) can whole tomatoes, undrained and chopped
1 teaspoon salt
¼ teaspoon pepper
Salt and pepper to taste

Rinse fish thoroughly in cold water; pat dry, and set aside.

Melt shortening in a large heavy skillet. Sauté potatoes until browned. Stir in green pepper, tomatoes, 1 teaspoon salt, and ¼ teaspoon pepper. Layer fish over vegetables. Cover and cook over high heat 5 minutes. Reduce heat to low; cover and simmer 15 minutes or until fish flakes easily when tested with a fork.

Arrange fish around outside of a serving platter; place vegetables in center of platter. Add salt and pepper to taste. Serve immediately. Yield: 4 servings.

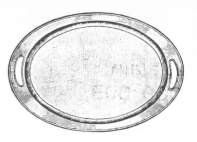

CRAPPIE PAYSANNE

1½ pounds crappie fillets
2 tablespoons lemon juice
½ teaspoon salt
¼ teaspoon pepper
1½ tablespoons butter or margarine, divided
2 medium carrots, thinly sliced
2 medium onions, thinly sliced
1 tablespoon chopped fresh parsley
1 cup white wine
1 tablespoon all-purpose flour
1 tablespoon butter or margarine, softened

Rinse fish thoroughly in cold water; pat dry. Brush fish with lemon juice; sprinkle with salt and pepper. Set aside.

Cut out a 9-inch circle of unglazed brown paper. (Do not use recycled paper.) Puncture paper once with a fork; grease heavily, and set aside.

Melt 1½ teaspoons butter in a 9-inch skillet; add carrots and onions. Cover, and cook over medium heat until vegetables are tender; uncover, and dot with 3 teaspoons butter. Place fish on top of vegetables; add parsley and wine. Cover skillet with prepared paper.

Bring mixture to a boil; reduce heat, and simmer 10 minutes or until fish flakes easily when tested with a fork. Transfer fish and vegetables to a warm serving platter, reserving wine sauce in skillet.

Combine flour and softened butter in a small mixing bowl; mix well, and stir into remaining wine sauce in skillet. Cook over low heat until thickened.

Pour wine sauce over fish and vegetables. Serve immediately. Yield: 2 to 4 servings.

Early twentieth-century photo combines feminine fashion with fishing.

FRIED PERCH

9 pan-dressed freshwater
   perch (about 3 pounds)
1 tablespoon salt
¾ teaspoon pepper
3 eggs, beaten
3 tablespoons milk
1½ cups cornmeal
Vegetable oil
Cocktail sauce or tartar
   sauce (page 126)

Rinse fish thoroughly in cold
water; pat dry. Sprinkle fish
with salt and pepper. Combine
eggs and milk in a medium mixing bowl. Dip fish in egg mixture; roll in cornmeal.

Fry in deep hot oil (375°) until
fish are golden brown. Drain
well on paper towels. Transfer
fish to a warm serving platter,
and serve immediately with
cocktail sauce or tartar sauce.
Yield: 4 servings.

SPICY BOILED PERCH

3 pounds pan-dressed
   freshwater perch
2 quarts water
1 large onion, peeled and
   coarsely chopped
1 bay leaf
Rind of 1 lemon, cut into
   pieces
2 cloves garlic, halved
2 teaspoons whole allspice
1 teaspoon dried whole
   thyme
1 teaspoon red pepper flakes
1 bunch fresh parsley
Lemon slices
Clarified butter (page 127)

Rinse fish thoroughly in cold
water; pat dry, and set aside.

Combine next 9 ingredients
in a large Dutch oven; bring to a
boil. Boil, uncovered, 10 minutes. Place fish in Dutch oven.
(Add additional hot water, if

necessary, to cover fish with liquid.) Simmer, uncovered, 8
minutes or until fish flakes easily when tested with a fork.

Carefully remove fish from liquid; drain. Discard cooking liquid. Arrange fish on a warm,
parsley-lined serving platter.
Garnish with lemon slices.
Serve with clarified butter.
Yield: 4 servings.

TROUT

BAKED TROUT

12 freshwater trout fillets
   (about 2 pounds)
4 eggs, beaten
1 cup Italian breadcrumbs
¼ cup butter or margarine
¼ teaspoon dried whole
   oregano
Paprika
Lemon wedges

Rinse fish thoroughly in cold water; pat dry. Soak fish in egg 10 minutes. Roll fish in breadcrumbs. Place fish, skin side down, in a 13- x 9- x 2-inch baking dish; dot with butter. Sprinkle with oregano and paprika.

Bake, uncovered, at 350° for 30 minutes or until fish flakes easily when tested with a fork. Transfer to a serving platter; garnish with lemon, and serve. Yield: 6 servings.

TROUT MARGUÉRY

8 (¼-pound) freshwater trout
   fillets
3 tablespoons olive oil
2 egg yolks, lightly beaten
1 tablespoon all-purpose flour
¼ cup butter, melted
¼ cup water
1 tablespoon lemon juice
½ teaspoon salt
¼ teaspoon pepper
¼ teaspoon paprika
20 medium shrimp, cooked,
   peeled, deveined, and
   chopped
½ cup lump crabmeat,
   drained and flaked
½ cup sliced fresh
   mushrooms

Rinse fish thoroughly in cold water; pat dry. Place fish, skin side down, on a 15- x 10- x 1-inch jellyroll pan; sprinkle fish with olive oil. Bake at 375° for 30 minutes or until fish flakes easily when tested with a fork. Remove fish to a warm serving platter; keep warm.

Combine egg yolks and flour in a medium saucepan; mix well. Gradually add butter, stirring until smooth. Add remaining ingredients; mix well. Cook over medium heat 3 minutes, stirring occasionally. Pour sauce over prepared fish, and serve immediately. Yield: 6 to 8 servings.

TROUT WITH HOLLANDAISE SHRIMP SAUCE

6 freshwater trout fillets
   (about 2 pounds)
½ teaspoon salt
¼ teaspoon pepper
3 tablespoons olive oil
¾ cup water
Hollandaise Shrimp
   Sauce

Rinse fish thoroughly in cold water; pat dry. Sprinkle fish with salt and pepper. Roll up each piece jellyroll fashion.

Place oil in bottom of a 9-inch square baking pan. Place fish rolls in pan, seam side down. Pour water in pan.

Bake, uncovered, at 400° for 35 minutes or until fish flakes easily when tested with a fork; baste frequently with liquid.

Transfer fish to a serving platter, seam side down. Pour Hollandaise Shrimp Sauce over top. Yield: 6 servings.

Hollandaise Shrimp Sauce:

3 egg yolks
1 tablespoon boiling water
3 tablespoons water
2 tablespoons warm lemon
   juice
½ cup butter, melted
¼ teaspoon salt
Pinch of red pepper
1 dozen medium shrimp,
   cooked, peeled, deveined,
   and coarsely chopped
½ (3-ounce) can sliced
   mushrooms, drained
¼ cup pineapple tidbits

Place yolks in top of a double boiler; place over simmering water. Beat yolks with a wire whisk until they begin to thicken. Add boiling water; beat again until egg mixture begins to thicken. Gradually add 3 tablespoons water, 1 tablespoon at a time, beating well after each addition. Add lemon juice, butter, salt, and pepper; beat until well blended.

Carefully fold in shrimp, mushrooms, and drained pineapple. Heat thoroughly, and serve immediately over fish rolls. Yield: about 1½ cups.

*Trout with Hollandaise
Shrimp Sauce*

BROILED TROUT FILLETS

8 freshwater trout fillets
  (about 1¾ pounds)
1 teaspoon salt
Dash of pepper
Dash of red pepper
½ cup butter or margarine,
  melted
2 teaspoons lemon juice
2 teaspoons Worcestershire
  sauce
Fresh parsley sprigs
Lemon slices

Rinse fish thoroughly in cold water; pat dry. Place skin side up in an aluminum foil-lined shallow baking pan; sprinkle with salt and pepper. Combine butter, lemon juice, and Worcestershire sauce; pour over fish.

Broil 4 to 5 inches from heating element 10 minutes or until fish flakes easily when tested with a fork; do not turn. Transfer fish to a serving platter. Garnish with parsley and lemon. Yield: 4 servings.

TROUT AMANDINE

2 dressed freshwater trout
  (about 1 pound)
¼ cup all-purpose flour
½ teaspoon salt
¼ teaspoon pepper
3 tablespoons Clarified
  butter, divided (page 127)
1 tablespoon lemon juice
2 tablespoons slivered
  almonds
Lemon slices
Chopped fresh parsley

Rinse fish thoroughly in cold water; pat dry, and set aside.

Combine flour, salt, and pepper in a small bowl; dredge fish in flour. Fry fish in 2 tablespoons clarified butter in a large skillet 5 minutes on each side or until golden brown. Transfer to a warm serving dish; sprinkle with lemon juice.

Add remaining clarified butter to skillet. Add almonds, and sauté until golden brown. Spoon almonds over fish. Garnish with lemon and parsley. Yield: 2 servings.

SAUTÉED TROUT

2 (¾-pound) dressed
  freshwater trout
½ cup all-purpose flour
3 tablespoons butter
Lemon slices (optional)

Rinse fish thoroughly in cold water; pat dry. Dredge fish in flour; shake off excess flour.

Sauté fish in 3 tablespoons butter in a large skillet over medium heat until golden brown, turning once. Drain fish well on paper towels, and transfer to a warm serving platter. Garnish with lemon slices, if desired. Yield: 2 servings.

Note: Sautéed Trout is delicious as a breakfast dish.

Caught on the Fly, a humorous Currier and Ives lithograph, 1879.

TROUT MEUNIÈRE

In 1496, de Worde's *Boke of St. Albans* described some handmade flies, but artificial lures of lint and feathers go back to 200 B.C. Fishing tackle today is highly specialized.

3 pounds freshwater trout fillets
½ cup all-purpose flour
1½ teaspoons salt
½ teaspoon white pepper
½ cup Clarified butter (page 127)
¼ cup chopped fresh parsley
¼ cup fresh squeezed lemon juice

Rinse fish thoroughly; pat dry, and set aside.

Combine ½ cup flour, salt, and pepper; dredge fish in flour mixture. Brown in clarified butter in a large skillet until fish flakes easily when tested with a fork. Remove fish to a warm serving platter; set aside. Reserve butter in skillet.

Cook butter over low heat, stirring constantly, until browned. Remove from heat, and pour over cooked fish; sprinkle with parsley and lemon juice. Serve immediately. Yield: 8 servings.

TROUT WITH ALMOND-LEMON SAUCE

12 freshwater trout fillets (about 2 pounds)
⅓ cup butter or margarine
1 cup lemon juice
½ cup chopped onion
¼ cup Worcestershire sauce
¼ cup chopped fresh parsley
½ cup sliced almonds
4 eggs, lightly beaten
1 cup milk
2 cups all-purpose flour
1 teaspoon pepper
Vegetable oil

Rinse fish thoroughly in cold water; pat dry, and set aside.

Combine butter, lemon juice, onion, and Worcestershire sauce in a saucepan; cook over medium heat, stirring occasionally, until butter melts. Stir in parsley and almonds. Remove from heat; keep warm.

Combine eggs and milk in a large mixing bowl; beat well. Dip fish in egg mixture; dredge in flour. Sprinkle with pepper.

Fry in ½ inch hot oil (350°) in a large skillet 3 minutes or until golden brown, turning once. (When done, fish should flake easily when tested with a fork.) Drain on paper towels.

Place fish on a warm serving platter; spoon almond-lemon sauce over top. Serve immediately. Yield: 6 servings.

Condensed coffee enhances a fishing trip, 1879 trade card.

FRIED TROUT NUGGETS

2½ pounds freshwater trout fillets
2 cups fine dry breadcrumbs
3 eggs, lightly beaten
½ cup milk
1 teaspoon salt
½ teaspoon pepper
3 tablespoons lard
Tartar sauce (page 126)

Rinse fish in cold water; pat dry. Cut fish into 2-inch squares. Roll each piece in breadcrumbs.

Combine eggs and milk in a medium mixing bowl. Dip each fish square into egg mixture. Roll in breadcrumbs again, and sprinkle with salt and pepper.

Heat lard in a large skillet to 350°; add trout nuggets, and fry 3 to 4 minutes or until golden brown, turning once. (When done, fish should flake easily when tested with a fork.) Drain well on paper towels.

Place trout nuggets on a warm serving platter. Serve immediately with tartar sauce. Yield: 6 to 8 servings.

MARINATED GRILLED TROUT

6 (¾-pound) dressed
  freshwater trout,
  butterflied
Marinade (recipe follows)
1 tablespoon chopped
  fresh chives
6 fresh thyme sprigs
6 lemon wedges

Rinse fish in cold water; pat dry. Place in a large mixing bowl; pour marinade over fish. Cover and refrigerate 4 hours or overnight.

Place open butterflied fillets on grill, skin-side down, 4 to 5 inches from hot coals. Sprinkle with chives; place thyme on fish. Lightly squeeze juice from lemon wedges onto fish, and lay wedges on top of each fish. Grill fish, without turning, 10 minutes or until fish flakes easily when tested with a fork. Baste frequently with marinade.

Transfer fish to a warm serving platter. Serve immediately. Yield: 6 servings.

Marinade:

1 cup vegetable oil
2 tablespoons grated
  Parmesan cheese
1 tablespoon plus 1 teaspoon
  salt
1½ teaspoons Worcestershire
  sauce
1½ teaspoons sugar
½ cup vinegar
2 tablespoons lemon juice

Combine first 5 ingredients in container of an electric blender; process 30 seconds. Add vinegar and lemon juice; process 30 seconds. Cover and chill until ready to use. Yield: 2 cups.

FRIED FISH BALLS

3 pounds freshwater trout
  fillets, cooked and flaked
½ cup finely chopped
  onion
½ cup finely chopped
  green pepper
1 tablespoon chopped
  fresh parsley
¼ cup lemon juice
¾ cup fine, dry breadcrumbs
2 eggs, beaten
½ cup milk
2 teaspoons spicy brown
  mustard
2 teaspoons salt
¼ teaspoon pepper
Vegetable oil
Cocktail sauce (page 126)

Combine first 11 ingredients in a large mixing bowl; mix well. Shape into 1-inch balls. (At this point, balls may be frozen; when ready to use, partially thaw and fry as directed below.)

Fry croquettes in 2-inch-deep hot oil (370°) until golden brown. Drain on paper towels. Serve immediately with cocktail sauce. Yield: 5½ dozen.

Note: This makes a delicious appetizer and may be made with any cooked fish.

TROUT SKILLET DINNER

½ cup all-purpose flour
1 teaspoon salt, divided
½ teaspoon pepper, divided
2 pounds trout fillets, cut
  into 6 serving-size portions
Vegetable oil
1 medium onion, thinly sliced
3 medium potatoes, parboiled,
  peeled, and sliced
1 (14½-ounce) can chopped
  tomatoes, undrained
2 tablespoons catsup
1 cup (4 ounces) shredded
  Cheddar cheese

Combine flour, ½ teaspoon salt, and ¼ teaspoon pepper in a large mixing bowl, stirring well. Dredge fish in flour mixture; set aside. Heat ¼ inch oil in a large skillet; add fish, and brown on both sides. Remove from heat; drain excess oil.

Place onion and potato slices over fish in skillet; set aside. Combine tomatoes, catsup, and remaining salt and pepper; pour over vegetables. Sprinkle with cheese; cover, and simmer 20 minutes or until onion is tender. Serve immediately from skillet. Yield: 6 servings.

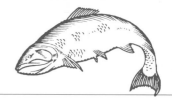

CEDARVALE GARDENS TROUT IDA

6 (¾-pound) dressed
  freshwater trout, butterflied
1 (16-ounce) bottle
  commercial Italian salad
  dressing
6 lemon wedges

Rinse fish in cold water; pat dry. Place in a large mixing bowl; pour salad dressing over fish. Cover and refrigerate 4 hours or overnight.

Place trout on grill, skin-side down, 4 to 5 inches from hot coals. Grill without turning 10 minutes or until fish flakes easily when tested with a fork.

Transfer fish to a warm serving platter. Garnish with lemon wedges. Serve immediately. Yield: 6 servings.

GRILLED TROUT

2 (¾-pound) dressed
  freshwater trout, butterflied
½ teaspoon salt
½ cup butter or margarine
2 tablespoons lemon juice
1½ tablespoons
  Worcestershire sauce
Vegetable oil

Rinse fish in cold water; pat dry. Sprinkle fish with salt. Place open butterflied fillets on a wire rack; place another wire rack on top. Secure racks with wires to clamp fish together (this will prevent fish from breaking apart during grilling).

Melt butter in a small saucepan; stir in lemon juice. Remove from heat, and stir in Worcestershire sauce. Set aside for basting.

Place fish on grill 4 to 5 inches from medium-hot coals. Baste once with oil. Grill 10 minutes or until fish flakes easily when tested with a fork, turning often. Baste frequently with butter mixture.

Carefully remove racks; place fish on a warm serving platter, and serve. Yield: 2 servings.

This tangle of hooks, lines, and youngsters took place in 1920 near Mechanicsville, Virginia.

SEASONING HIGHLIGHTS

"Salmon is so fine a fish," confided Miss Eliza Leslie of Philadelphia in her *New Cookery Book* of 1857, "that its own flavor is better than any that can be communicated except by the most simple sauce." She recommended cold butter spread over the cooked fish, then, with growing enthusiasm, launched into sauces compounded of minced shrimp or lobster and rich cream reminiscent of the French-born sauce that goes into Pompano *en Papillote* of New Orleans fame.

It had taken over two centuries and several generations for Americans to come to terms with the plethora of seafood lapping the shores. The tribal English craving for meat, not fish, with or without sauce, was at the core of the difficulty. Eels and salt cod were exceptions; the settlers were accustomed to them. But as late as 1740, an English visitor wrote home from Boston that a fourteen-pound salmon cost only a shilling. Penny-apiece salmon and shad shared the bottom rung in the South as well.

Mary Randolph's *Virginia Housewife*, 1824, dwelt heavily upon salt fish (with egg sauce), but the tide had started to turn: Shad came in for four treatments, one of which was to bake it attentively in red wine and mushroom catsup, the juices thickened with brown flour. Oysters were used in sauce or stuffing for fish or fried to garnish calves' head.

Shellfish were not ordinarily sauced; they became sauce. (Large lobster was an exception; Americans had recovered from their embarrassment at eating it.) Miss Leslie on shrimp: "At good tables they are used as sauce for large fish, squeezed out of the shell and stirred into melted butter." On crab: "They are very abundant, but so little is in them that when better things are to be had, they are scarcely worth the trouble of boiling and picking out of the shell." Nevertheless, she sauced fried soft-shell crab with fried lettuce and peppered cream gravy for a breakfast dish.

Cooks had begun to use marinades: herbed cream with sheepshead (drum) and tomato with sea bass. By the late 1800s, the marinades, stocks, and sauces we use now were formed or forming.

Some of our best seafood sauces (clockwise from front): Cucumber Sauce, Dill and Mustard Sauce, Orange Basting Sauce, Remoulade Sauce, and Seafood Cocktail Sauce.

SEAFOOD COCKTAIL SAUCE

1½ cups catsup
2 tablespoons prepared
  horseradish
1 tablespoon lemon
  juice
1 tablespoon Worcestershire
  sauce
1½ teaspoons sugar
¼ teaspoon salt
⅛ teaspoon pepper
Dash of hot sauce

Combine all ingredients in a small mixing bowl, mixing well. Cover mixture, and chill several hours to blend flavors. Serve sauce cold with seafood or shellfish. Yield: about 1¾ cups.

Above: *Trade card for Snider condiments, c.1900.* Below: *The catsup bottling works of the Beechnut Packing Company, 1927.*

National Archives

TARTAR SAUCE

1 cup mayonnaise
½ cup sweet pickle
  relish
¼ cup finely chopped
  onion

Combine all ingredients in a small mixing bowl; stir well. Cover and chill at least 2 hours to blend flavors. Serve sauce cold with fish or seafood. Yield: 1½ cups.

SOUR CREAM TARTAR SAUCE

1 cup mayonnaise
½ cup commercial sour
  cream
2 tablespoons finely
  chopped dill pickle
1 tablespoon finely
  chopped onion
1 tablespoon finely chopped
  fresh parsley
1 tablespoon lemon
  juice
¼ teaspoon dried whole
  thyme
¼ teaspoon dried whole
  tarragon
⅛ teaspoon pepper

Combine all ingredients in a small mixing bowl, mixing well. Cover mixture, and chill overnight to blend flavors. Serve sauce cold with fish or seafood. Yield: 1¾ cups.

HOMEMADE MAYONNAISE

3 egg yolks
1 teaspoon salt
2 cups vegetable oil
2 tablespoons white vinegar

Beat yolks and salt in a deep, narrow bowl at high speed of an electric mixer until thick and lemon colored. Add oil in a thin, steady stream; beat until mixture begins to thicken. Gradually add vinegar, beating until thickened.

Spoon mayonnaise into a glass or plastic container; cover container and refrigerate. Yield: about 2 cups.

CUCUMBER SAUCE

½ cup finely chopped, peeled cucumber
1 cup mayonnaise
3 tablespoons lemon juice
¼ teaspoon curry powder
Dash of hot sauce

Pat cucumber between paper towels to remove moisture, and set aside.

Combine remaining ingredients in a small mixing bowl. Stir cucumber into mayonnaise mixture; mix well. Cover; chill thoroughly before serving. Serve sauce cold with poached fish. Yield: 1½ cups.

REMOULADE SAUCE

2 cups mayonnaise
2 hard-cooked eggs, finely chopped
2 cloves garlic, crushed
1 tablespoon drained capers
1 tablespoon minced fresh parsley
½ teaspoon dry mustard
½ teaspoon dried tarragon leaves
½ teaspoon anchovy paste

Combine all ingredients in a mixing bowl; stir well. Cover and refrigerate at least 3 hours. Serve sauce cold with poached fish or with chilled boiled shrimp. Yield: 2½ cups.

CLARIFIED BUTTER

1 cup butter

Melt butter in a small saucepan over low heat without stirring. Remove from heat, and let stand 10 minutes. The butter will separate and the milk solids will settle to the bottom of the saucepan.

Skim the butter fat from the top; discard milk solids. Place several layers of cheesecloth in a strainer; strain butter fat through cheesecloth into a small bowl. Yield: about ½ cup.

Note: Clarified butter is also referred to as drawn butter.

MAÎTRE D'HÔTEL BUTTER

½ cup butter, softened
½ teaspoon salt
⅛ teaspoon pepper
1 tablespoon chopped fresh parsley
1 tablespoon lemon juice

Cream butter in a small mixing bowl. Add salt, pepper, parsley, and lemon juice; stir well. Store mixture in a covered container in refrigerator until ready to use. Serve butter at room temperature with pompano or other baked or broiled fish. Yield: ½ cup.

Trade card for Heinz's Keystone Pickles, c.1890.

A crab net completes the Mardi Gras costume, c.1890.

BÉARNAISE SAUCE

2½ tablespoons Chablis or
   other dry white wine
2½ tablespoons red wine
   vinegar
1 tablespoon minced shallots
½ teaspoon dried chervil
   leaves
½ teaspoon dried tarragon
   leaves
¼ teaspoon white pepper
3 egg yolks
2 tablespoons water
½ cup butter, melted
¼ cup chopped fresh parsley
1 teaspoon lemon juice
Dash of salt and pepper

Combine first 6 ingredients in
a small saucepan; bring to a
boil. Reduce heat to low, and
simmer until liquid is reduced
by half; cool.

Beat yolks and water in top of
a double boiler with a wire
whisk. Gradually add vinegar
mixture, beating well. Place over
simmering water and cook,
beating constantly with wire
whisk, until mixture thickens.

Remove from heat, and add
butter, 1 tablespoon at a time,
beating constantly, until sauce
is smooth and thickened. Stir in
parsley, lemon juice, and salt
and pepper. Serve warm with
baked or broiled fish or shellfish. Yield: ¾ cup.

LEMON SAUCE

Juice of 1 lemon
¼ cup butter, softened
¼ teaspoon salt
⅛ teaspoon pepper
1 egg yolk

Combine lemon juice, butter,
salt, and pepper in a small
saucepan. Cook over medium
heat, beating with a wire whisk,
until butter melts and all ingredients are well blended.

Add a small amount of hot
mixture to yolk; stir well, and
add to remaining hot mixture.
Cook over low heat, beating
well, until mixture is smooth
and slightly thickened. Serve
immediately with baked or
broiled fish. Yield: about ½ cup.

BEURRE BLANC

1¼ cups butter
¼ cup red wine vinegar
¼ cup vermouth
2 tablespoons lemon juice
2 tablespoons chopped
   shallots
½ teaspoon salt
¼ teaspoon pepper

Cut butter into 14 equal portions. Set butter portions aside
to soften.

Combine remaining ingre-
dients in a small saucepan.
Cook over high heat, stirring occasionally, until mixture is reduced to 1½ tablespoons.

Add portions of butter, one at
a time, to reduced cooking liquid, beating constantly with a
wire whisk until butter melts and
mixture turns white. Re-
move from heat. Serve immediately with baked or broiled fish.
Yield: about 1 cup.

HOLLANDAISE SAUCE

½ cup butter, slightly
   softened
2 egg yolks
1 tablespoon lemon juice
¼ teaspoon salt
Dash of red pepper

Cut butter into 3 equal portions. Combine 1 portion butter, yolks, and lemon juice in
top of a double boiler. Cream together, using a fork, until mixture is smooth.

Place over simmering water,
and cook, beating constantly
with a wire whisk, until butter
begins to melt. Continue to add
butter, one portion at a time,
beating constantly, until sauce
is smooth and thickened. Lift
top of double boiler from water
occasionally. Remove from heat,
and stir in salt and pepper.
Serve immediately with baked
or broiled fish. Yield: ½ cup.

EGG SAUCE

3 tablespoons butter or
  margarine
2 tablespoons all-purpose
  flour
1 cup Court Bouillon (page
  132)
1 hard-cooked egg, chopped
¼ teaspoon salt
⅛ teaspoon pepper

Melt butter in a heavy sauce-pan over low heat; add flour, stirring until smooth. Cook 1 minute, stirring constantly. Gradually add Court Bouillon; cook over medium heat, stirring constantly, until mixture is thickened and bubbly. Stir in egg, salt, and pepper. Serve sauce immediately over baked fish. Yield: about 1 cup.

DILL AND MUSTARD SAUCE

2 to 2½ tablespoons dry
  mustard
¼ cup plus 1 tablespoon
  sugar
½ teaspoon salt
2 tablespoons vegetable oil
1 tablespoon vinegar
½ cup commercial sour
  cream
2 tablespoons fresh dillweed,
  chopped

Combine mustard, sugar, and salt; mix well. Add oil and vinegar alternately, beating until well blended. Fold in sour cream and dillweed. Cover and chill thoroughly. Serve sauce cold with cold crab claws or other chilled shellfish. Yield: 1 cup.

SAUCE PIQUANT

1 hot red pepper, finely
  chopped
1 tablespoon minced onion
1 tablespoon chopped fresh
  parsley
3 tablespoons vegetable oil
1 tablespoon vinegar
1 teaspoon prepared mustard
⅛ teaspoon salt

Combine all ingredients, mixing well. Serve sauce with any fried fish. Yield: about ⅓ cup.

CAPER SAUCE

½ cup butter or margarine,
  divided
3 tablespoons all-purpose
  flour
½ teaspoon salt
⅛ teaspoon pepper
1½ cups hot water
1 teaspoon lemon juice
1 (3-ounce) jar capers,
  drained

Melt ¼ cup butter in a heavy saucepan over low heat. Add flour, salt, and pepper, stirring until smooth. Cook 1 minute, stirring constantly. Gradually add water; cook over medium heat, stirring constantly, until thickened and bubbly.

Gradually stir in lemon juice and remaining butter, beating constantly, until butter is well blended. Add capers, stirring well. Serve sauce warm over baked or broiled pompano. Yield: 2 cups.

Trade card for Stickney and Poors Mustard, c.1890.

Collection of Kit Barry

129

OYSTER SAUCE

1 (12-ounce) container
Standard oysters, undrained
Milk
3 tablespoons butter or
margarine
3 tablespoons all-purpose
flour
½ teaspoon salt
¼ teaspoon pepper
1 teaspoon minced fresh
parsley
1 teaspoon minced onion

Place oysters in a medium-size heavy saucepan; parboil in oyster liquor 3 minutes or until oysters become plump and edges begin to curl. Remove oysters from liquor, and set aside to drain on paper towels. Pour oyster liquor into a 2-cup glass measure; add milk to equal 2 cups. Set aside.

Melt butter in saucepan over low heat; add flour, stirring until smooth. Cook 1 minute, stirring constantly. Gradually add reserved oyster liquor mixture; cook over medium heat, stirring constantly, until thickened and bubbly. Stir in salt, pepper, reserved oysters, parsley, and onion. Serve sauce hot with baked fish. Yield: 2½ cups.

SPANISH SAUCE

3 medium onions, chopped
1 small green pepper,
chopped
1 tablespoon vegetable oil
1 (14½-ounce) can whole
tomatoes, undrained and
chopped
1 cup cooked green peas
¼ teaspoon salt
Dash of red pepper

Sauté onion and green pepper in oil in a large skillet; add tomatoes, peas, salt, and pepper, stirring well. Cook over medium heat, stirring frequently, until thoroughly heated. Serve sauce hot over baked, fried, or broiled fish. Yield: about 3 cups.

TOMATO SAUCE

½ cup finely chopped onion
2 tablespoons butter or
margarine
2 cups chopped tomatoes
½ cup water
2 tablespoons chopped fresh
parsley
¼ teaspoon paprika
1 teaspoon salt
⅛ teaspoon white pepper
1 tablespoon cornstarch

Sauté onion in butter in a large skillet until tender. Add tomatoes, water, parsley, paprika, salt, and pepper; cook over medium heat 5 minutes. Remove from heat. Strain mixture through a sieve; discard vegetables. Return strained liquid to skillet; bring to a boil. Reduce heat to low.

Combine cornstarch and a small amount of water to form a smooth paste. Stir into strained liquid. Cook mixture, stirring constantly, 1 minute or until thickened and bubbly. Serve sauce hot with baked fish. Yield: 1½ cups.

A tender moment in the history of advertising: A portrait of "Mother" on an oyster shell advertising Baltimore Oysters, c.1890.

New Hanover County Museum of the Lower Cape Fear

OLD SOUR SAUCE

3 cups lime juice
1 tablespoon salt
4 medium-size hot red
 peppers

Combine lime juice and salt in a clear glass jar, stirring until salt dissolves. Add peppers; cover and let sit in the sunshine 2 days. Remove and discard peppers; bottle sauce. Refrigerate. Serve with baked, broiled, or fried fish. Yield: 3 cups.

Note: Old Sour is highly concentrated and should be used sparingly.

SWEET-AND-SOUR SAUCE

½ cup honey
½ cup prepared mustard
½ cup cider vinegar
¼ cup Worcestershire sauce
2 teaspoons hot sauce
1 teaspoon salt
1 tablespoon chopped fresh
 parsley

Combine all ingredients in a small saucepan; stir well. Bring to a boil. Remove from heat. Serve hot with smoked mullet. Yield: 1¾ cups.

FISH BASTING SAUCE

⅓ cup Chablis or other dry
 white wine
⅓ cup lemon juice
⅓ cup butter or margarine

Combine all ingredients in a small saucepan; simmer, stirring occasionally, until butter melts. Use sauce to baste fish during baking, broiling, or grilling procedure. Yield: 1 cup.

Tintype portrait, c.1880.

A lakeside picnic on Lake Waccamaw, Columbus County, North Carolina, 1901. Steam launch in background.

TROPICAL BASTING SAUCE

½ cup butter or margarine
¼ cup lemon juice
¼ cup pineapple juice
1 tablespoon garlic powder
1 teaspoon dried parsley
 flakes

Combine all ingredients in a small saucepan. Cook over medium heat, stirring occasionally, until butter melts. Use sauce to baste fish during grilling procedure. Yield: 1 cup.

ORANGE BASTING SAUCE

½ cup butter or margarine
½ teaspoon grated orange
 rind
½ cup freshly squeezed
 orange juice

Melt butter in a small saucepan over medium heat. Stir in orange rind and juice. Use sauce to baste fish during broiling procedure. Yield: 1 cup.

SEAFOOD MARINADE SAUCE

½ cup butter or margarine
¼ cup lemon juice
2½ tablespoons Dijon mustard
1 tablespoon dill pickle juice
1 tablespoon soy sauce
1 tablespoon garlic powder
1 tablespoon liquid crab and shrimp boil

Melt butter in a small sauce-pan over low heat; remove from heat, and add remaining ingredients, mixing well. Cool. Use sauce as a marinade for seafood. Yield: 1¼ cups.

For an entrée of exceptional taste, soak salmon steaks in Spicy Seafood Marinade before popping it in the oven.

SPICY SEAFOOD MARINADE

¼ cup butter or margarine
½ cup Chablis or other dry white wine
½ teaspoon prepared mustard
½ teaspoon salt
¼ teaspoon lemon and pepper seasoning
¼ teaspoon seafood seasoning
⅛ teaspoon dried whole tarragon
⅛ teaspoon dried whole rosemary

Melt butter in a small sauce-pan over low heat. Add wine, mustard, and seasonings, stirring well. Cook over low heat, stirring occasionally, 10 minutes or until mixture is well blended and thoroughly heated. Use sauce as a marinade for fish or shrimp. Yield: ⅔ cup.

Mr. Oliver of Birmingham, proudly displays his 215-pound tarpon caught off the Rolston Hotel at Coden, Alabama, 1916.

BASIC FISH STOCK

1½ to 2 pounds fish trimmings (bones, head, and skin)
2 medium onions, thinly sliced
1 cup Chablis or other dry white wine
Juice of 1 medium lemon
6 stems fresh parsley (do not use leaves)
1 bay leaf
¼ teaspoon salt
⅛ teaspoon white pepper

Combine all ingredients in a medium Dutch oven; cover with water. Simmer, uncovered, 30 minutes, skimming surface of stock frequently.

Strain stock into a large bowl, discarding fish trimmings and vegetables. Cool to room temperature. Skim clear stock, discarding sediment remaining in bottom of bowl. Cover; refrigerate until ready to use. Use as a base for poaching fish or to flavor fish sauces and soups. Yield: about 2 cups.

COURT BOUILLON

Head and bones of 1 fish
2 cups cold water
3 slices carrot
1 slice onion
1 sprig fresh parsley
2 tablespoons lemon juice
½ small bay leaf
¼ teaspoon peppercorns
1 teaspoon salt

Combine all ingredients in a medium saucepan. Bring to a boil, and cook 20 minutes or until liquid is reduced to 1 cup. Strain, reserving liquid; discard fish trimmings and vegetables. Cover and refrigerate. Use to flavor fish aspic, sauces, or soups. Yield: 1 cup.

TARPON 215 LB. LENGTH-6'11"
GIRTH 43" CAUGHT OFF
ROLSTON HOTEL, CODEN, ALA.
BY MR. WG OLIVER. B'HAM. 8/31/16

HOW TO STEAK OR FILLET A FISH

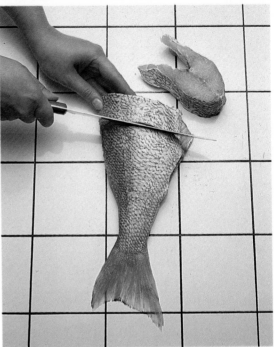

To steak a fish: *Step 1—Remove head by cutting through body behind the pectoral fins of an eviscerated fish. Trim fins close to body; discard head and fins.*

Step 2—*Beginning at the head end, cut 1-inch-wide slices completely through fish. A hammer or mallet may be used to tap the knife through the backbone.*

To fillet a fish: *Step 1—Make a short diagonal cut down to the backbone behind the pectoral fin. Make a shallow cut from head to tail just above the dorsal fin. Begin cutting away the fillet by running the blade along the top of the backbone.*

Step 2—*Continue carefully cutting the fillet away from the skeleton along the top of the backbone. Cut around the bony area of the belly cavity. Turn the fish over and repeat the filleting procedure shown in step 1. Discard skeleton of fish.*

GOOD
TO KNOW

SELECTING QUALITY FISH AND SHELLFISH

Fish and shellfish must be handled properly from the time they are harvested until ready for cooking and eating. Whether fresh, frozen, or canned, the package should indicate the quality of the product.

- Check all fish and shellfish for freshness and quality before purchasing. Inspection labels on packages will indicate that the product is wholesome and has been processed under sanitary conditions.
- A U.S. Grade A shield on the package will indicate that it contains the very best quality fish and shellfish.
- Regardless of the type of fish or shellfish, it is important that it be refrigerated at all times.

FRESH FISH

Whole fish can be easily judged for freshness if you know the characteristics of good quality fish. A quick check of the eyes, gills, scales and skin, flesh, and odor will indicate the freshness of the fish. The eyes should be bright, clear, and bulging. The gills should be red or pink and fresh-smelling. The scales should be bright, shiny, and tight to the skin; the skin should be irridescent and unfaded. The flesh should feel firm and elastic; it should spring back when pressed with the finger. The fish should emit a mild, fresh odor. A strong or "fishy" odor is a good indication that the fish is not fresh.

Some of the same characteristics can be used when judging the freshness of fish which have been dressed or cut into fillets or steaks. The flesh should be firm and elastic. There should be no indication of browning or drying around the edges. The fish should emit a mild, fresh odor.

Fresh fish may be purchased in a variety of market forms:

Whole or Round: The whole fish as it comes from the water. Before cooking, the fish must be eviscerated (internal organs removed) and scaled. Usually the head, tail, and fins are removed.

Drawn: The whole fish which has been eviscerated. The scales, head, fins, and tail are removed before cooking.

Whole-dressed: The whole fish which has been eviscerated and scaled. The head, tail, and fins remain intact.

Dressed or Pan-dressed: The whole fish which has been eviscerated. The head, tail, and fins have been removed. Smaller fish are usually pan-dressed.

Steaks: Cross-section slices (¾- to 1-inch thick) cut from large dressed fish. The only bone is a cross-section of the backbone and ribs.

Fillets: The sides of the fish cut lengthwise away from the backbone. When properly prepared, fillets are free of bones. They may or may not have the skin left on them.

Butterfly Fillets: The sides or fillets of the fish held together by the uncut belly skin.

FRESH SHELLFISH

When selecting fresh shellfish it is important to know the specific characteristics of each variety of shellfish.

Fresh clams in the shell should be alive when purchased. The shell will be tightly closed or should close quickly when tapped. Clams that will not close or that have cracked or broken shells should be discarded. Shucked clams should be plump. Any liquid should be clear.

Crabs and lobsters which are purchased alive should move their legs when touched. A live lobster will curl its tail under its body. Crabs and lobsters cooked in the shell should be bright red in color and emit no disagreeable odor.

Oysters in the shell, like clams, should be alive when purchased. Check to see that the shell is tightly closed or that it closes quickly when tapped. Oysters that will not close should be discarded. Shucked oysters should be plump and creamy in color. The liquid should be clear and not excessive.

Fresh scallops come in a variety of colors from white to orange. They should be packed in little or no free liquid and emit a sweet odor.

Fresh shrimp purchased in the shell will vary in color from gray to pink, depending on the variety. The meat should be firm and attached to the shell and should emit a mild odor. Fresh shrimp should be washed thoroughly in cold water immediately after purchasing and stored in the refrigerator.

PURCHASING

Consider the recipe, cooking method, and number of people to be served when purchasing fish or shellfish.

FRESH FISH

Whole or drawn fish: Allow 1 pound per serving.

Dressed fish: Allow ½ pound per serving.

Steaks or fillets: Allow ⅓ pound per serving.

SHELLFISH

Fresh clams: Allow 1 dozen clams in the shell per serving.

Fresh crab: Allow 3 to 4 whole crabs in the shell per serving.

Fresh lobster: Allow 1 pound lobster in the shell per serving.

Fresh oysters: Allow 1 dozen oysters in the shell per serving.

Fresh scallops: Allow ⅓ pound scallops per serving.

Fresh shrimp: Allow ½ pound shrimp in the shell per serving.

REFRIGERATION AND FREEZING

Fish and shellfish are extremely perishable and must be stored at safe temperatures. Fresh fish and shellfish should be carefully wrapped and kept under refrigeration at all times at temperatures between 31° and 32°F.

Although not absolutely necessary, whole, drawn, or dressed fish may be packed in finely crushed ice. Steaks or fillets however, should be wrapped in waxed paper before storing on ice.

Fish are best if cooked the day of purchase, but may be stored in the coldest part of the refrigerator for two days.

Prepackaged frozen fish should be kept frozen at or below 0°F. Care should be taken so that the fish does not thaw and refreeze during storage since this will affect the quality of the fish.

Loading Ice on Fish Boats, Pensacola, Fla.

The Pensacola Historical Society

The length of freezer storage will depend on the type and fat content of the fish.

Fresh fish which has been frozen should be thawed in the refrigerator prior to cooking. When thawing in the refrigerator, leave the fish in the original wrapper. If time is a factor, the fish may be placed in the wrapper under cold running water. Thawed fish should never be refrozen and should be cooked within one day after thawing.

The length of time which fresh shellfish may be refrigerated varies with the variety. It is a good practice to use fresh shellfish within 1 to 2 days of purchase.

COOKING METHODS

In order to determine how to cook fish properly, it is important to know whether the fish is fat or lean. A general rule to follow is the darker the color of the flesh of the fish, the higher the natural fat content and the more distinct the flavor. Fish such as mackerel, mullet, and tuna contain a high percentage of fat. Fish such as flounder, grouper, and snapper have a whiter color flesh, a lower percentage of fat, and a more delicate flavor. Although both fat and lean fish can be cooked using a variety of basic cooking methods, lean fish require that more fat or oil be added during cooking to keep the fish moist and flavorful.

Overcooking and cooking at too high temperatures are the most common problems associated with cooking fish. These factors tend to dry and toughen the fish and destroy the flavor. It is important to check the fish for doneness during the cooking procedure. To check for doneness, pierce the thickest part of the flesh with a fork. The flesh will flake easily, will lose its translucent appearance, and become opaque when it has reached the optimum degree of doneness.

A variety of cooking methods may be used for cooking fish and shellfish:

Baking: Place the fish in a greased baking dish. Keep the fish moist and flavorful with melted fat or a sauce. Bake at 350°F until the fish flakes easily when tested with a fork. Cooking time varies according to the thickness of the whole fish, steak, or fillet. However, approximately 10 minutes per inch thickness is a general rule for cooking thawed fish.

Broiling: Choose pan-dressed fish, fillets, or steaks. Place pan-dressed fish, fillets, or steaks in a single layer on a well-greased baking pan. Baste the fish well with melted fat or a basting sauce before and during cooking. The surface of the fish should be 3 to 4 inches from the heating element. Cooking time is usually 8 to 10 minutes. Thicker pieces of fish, such as pan-dressed fish, should be turned and basted halfway through the cooking time.

Pan-frying: Pan-frying involves cooking fish in a small amount of hot oil. Heat 1/8-inch oil in the bottom of a heavy skillet, and place breaded fish in a single layer in the hot oil. Do not overload the pan. Fry fish at a moderate temperature until lightly browned on one side; turn and lightly brown the other side, allowing 8 to 10 minutes cooking time.

Deep-fat frying: Deep-fat frying involves cooking fish in a deep layer of hot oil. Do not fill the cooking container more than half full of oil to allow room for fish and bubbling oil. Bring oil to frying temperature (370°). Lower breaded or battered fish slowly into hot oil. Fry until the fish is lightly browned and flakes easily when tested with a fork.

Grilling: Pan-dressed fish, fillets, or steaks may be cooked over hot coals. A well-greased, long-handled hinged wire grilling basket is recommended for ease in turning. Baste fish with sauce before and during grilling. Grill 4 inches from hot coals 10 to 20 minutes, depending on the thickness of the fish, turning halfway through grilling time. The fish is done when it flakes easily when tested with a fork.

Smoking: Use a covered charcoal, electric or gas grill, or smoker. The smoky flavor is obtained by adding water-soaked wood chips to the briquettes. The fish is placed on the grill, skin side down, and basted frequently during cooking. The fish is done when it flakes easily when tested with a fork. Cooking time varies with weather, intensity of heat, amount of moisture in chips, type of grill, distance of fish from heat, and variety of fish.

Simmering: Although shrimp and other seafood is generally referred to as "boiled," it should never be allowed to boil. Shellfish and fish are simmered when they are to be served with a sauce or flaked and combined with other ingredients. Bring salted water to a rolling boil in a large stockpot. Add the fish or shellfish; reduce heat, and simmer. The cooking time will vary according to the type of fish or shellfish.

Poaching: Poaching is cooking food in a simmering liquid. Place the fish in a single layer in a wide, shallow pan such as a skillet or roasting pan. Barely cover fish with a liquid such as water, milk, wine, or court bouillon. Simmer 5 to 7 minutes or until fish flakes easily when tested with a fork.

Steaming: Steaming is a delicate way to cook fish. Use a deep pan with a tight cover. If a steam cooker is not available, anything that prevents the fish from touching the water will serve as a steaming rack. The water may be plain or seasoned with various spices. Bring water to a rapid boil; place fish on the rack. Cover pan tightly, and steam 5 to 8 minutes or until the fish flakes easily when tested with a fork.

cACKNOWLEDGMENTS

Baked Bass adapted from *The Huntsville Heritage Cookbook* by The Grace Club Auxiliary, Inc., ©1967. By permission of The Grace Club Auxiliary, Inc., Huntsville, Alabama.

Baked Bass Fillets, Grilled Trout, Fried Fish Balls courtesy of Susan Jensen, Auburn, Alabama.

Baked Grouper with Lemon Stuffing, Catfish Stew, Florida Seatrout, Key West Conch Chowder, Marinated King Mackerel Steaks, Mullet Fillets with Shrimp Stuffing, Pompano Jacques Latour, Peck Smith's Fried Mullet, Red Snapper Floridian adapted from *Jane Nickerson's Florida Cookbook*, ©1973. By permission of University Presses of Florida, Gainesville.

Baked Stuffed Bluefish adapted from *Maryland Seafood Cookbook III* by the Seafood Marketing Authority, Department of Economic and Community Development, Annapolis.

Baked Stuffed Redfish, Catfish in Mushroom Cream Sauce adapted from *The Jackson Cookbook* by The Symphony League of Jackson, ©1971. By permission of The Symphony League of Jackson, Mississippi.

Bass Bake adapted from *Revel* by The Junior League of Shreveport, Inc., ©1980. By permission of Books Unlimited, Shreveport, Louisiana.

Bayley's Original West Indies Salad courtesy of Bayley's Catering Service, Dauphin Island Parkway, Theodore, Alabama.

Bluffton Seafood Boil, Broiled Oysters, Wilmington Island Baked Bass adapted from *Savannah Sampler Cookbook* by Margaret Wayt DeBolt, ©1978. By permission of Donning Company/Publishers, Norfolk, Virginia.

Boiled Crayfish, Crayfish Étouffée, Crayfish Jambalaya, Crayfish Pie courtesy of Chez Marcelle, Broussard, Louisiana.

Busters Béarnaise, New Orleans Bouillabaisse adapted from *Brennan's New Orleans Cookbook* by David C. Wilson, ©1961. By permission of Brennan's Restaurant, New Orleans.

Capt'n Buddy's Favorite, Grilled Bluefish, Grouper Italiano, Grouper Kabobs, Grouper with Spanish Sauce, Oyster Pie Rappahannock, Seaside Poached Bluefish adapted from recipes by the Virginia Marine Commission, Richmond, Virginia.

Catfish Étouffée, Oysters Bienville, Flounder en Papillote adapted from *Talk About Good!* by The Junior League of Lafayette, ©1969. By permission of The Junior League of Lafayette, Louisiana.

Cedarvale Garden's Trout Ida courtesy of Elaine Howell, Davis, Oklahoma.

Chesapeake House Crab Cakes adapted from *An Eastern Shore Sampler*, published in Delaware.

Clam Chowder, Steamed Oysters adapted from *Maryland Seafood Cookbook II* by the Seafood Marketing Authority, Department of Economic and Community Development, Annapolis.

Commander's Palace Crabmeat Imperial courtesy of Commander's Palace, New Orleans, Louisiana.

Crab Feast and Oyster Roast recipes courtesy of and prepared for photography by the Office of Seafood Marketing, Department of Economic and Community Development, Annapolis, Maryland.

Crabmeat Soufflé, Ybor City Crab Croquettes adapted from *The Southern Cookbook* by Marion Brown, ©1951. By permission of the University of North Carolina Press, Chapel Hill.

Crabmeat with Curried Rice, Henry's Restaurant Pompano à la Gherardi, Otranto Pine Bark Stew, Planked Shad, Shrimp Paste adapted from *Charleston Receipts* by The Junior League of Charleston, ©1950. By permission of The Junior League of Charleston, South Carolina.

Crab Sauce Lorenzo, by Mrs. W.J. Williamson, first appeared in *The Gasparilla Cookbook* by The Junior League of Tampa, ©1961. By permission of The Junior League of Tampa.

Daphne Lodge Fried Catfish and Hush Puppies courtesy of Daphne Lodge, Cordele, Georgia.

Flounder Stuffed with Crab, Broiled Flounder with Mushroom-Wine Sauce adapted from recipes by The Virginia Institute of Marine Science.

Fried Catfish Sandwiches courtesy of Armon Nash, owner, Cookville Boat Dock, Cookville, Tennessee.

Fried Chesapeake Bay Soft-Shell Crabs, Clams Casino adapted from *Chesapeake Bay Clam Recipes*, published in Annapolis, Maryland.

Grilled Soft-Shell Crabs, Seafood Marinade adapted from *Chesapeake Bay Crab Recipes*, published in Annapolis, Maryland.

Haddock Loaf adapted from *The Melting Pot: Ethnic Cuisine in Texas* by The Institute of Texan Culture, ©1977. By permission of The University of Texas Institute of Texan Cultures, San Antonio, Texas.

King Mackerel Steaks with Tomato-Wine Sauce adapted from *Florida Finfish Recipes* by the Florida Department of Natural Resources.

Linguine with White Clam Sauce adapted from *Magic* by The Junior League of Birmingham, ©1982. By permission of The Junior League of Birmingham, Alabama.

Louisville Rolled Oysters adapted from *Out of Kentucky Kitchens* by Marion Flexner, ©1949. By permission of Franklin Watts, Inc., New York.

Low Country Seafood Casserole courtesy of Mrs. John William Brabham, Charleston, South Carolina.

Old-Timer's Beer 'N' Bream, Skillet Crappie adapted from *Wild 'N Tame, Fish 'N Game* by Lynn Mitchell Moore, ©1981. By permission of Richard Moore, Inc., Cypress, Texas.

Orange Steamed Black Bass adapted from *The Encyclopedia of Fish Cookery* by A.J. McClane, ©1977. By permission of Holt, Rhinehart & Winston, New York.

Pickled Shrimp adapted from *Harris County Heritage Cookbook* by The Harris County Heritage Society. By permission of The Harris County Heritage Society, Houston, Texas.

Pirates' House Shrimp Pilau, Shrimp Fritters adapted from *The Pirates' House Cook Book*. Courtesy of Pirates' House Restaurant, Savannah, Georgia, publisher of the new *Pirates' House Cook Book* by Sarah Gaede, ©1982.

Salmon Mousse courtesy of Mayor Richard Arrington, Birmingham, Alabama.

Scallops au Gratin adapted from *Favorite Recipes From the Big House* by the N.G. Davis Family, ©1981. By permission of Cookbook Publishers, Inc., Lenexa Kansas.

She-Crab Soup adapted from *The South Carolina Cookbook*, edited by the South Carolina Extension Homemakers Council and the Clemson Extension Home Economics Staff. By permission of The University of South Carolina Press, Columbia, South Carolina.

Shrimp Creole courtesy of Marie Spiess, Opelousas, Louisiana.

Shrimp Gravy courtesy of Mills B. Lane, Savannah, Georgia.

Smokehouse Oysters adapted from *Outdoor Seafood Smoking* by the Florida Department of Natural Resources.

Steamed Blue Crabs, Steamed Clams adapted from *Maryland Seafood Cookbook I* by the Seafood Marketing Authority, Department of Economic and Community Development, Annapolis.

Swordfish Supreme adapted from *Hooked on Seafood* by Nana Whalen, ©1982. By permission of WRC Publishing, Silver Spring, Maryland.

The Homestead Shrimp Creole Fricassee courtesy of The Homestead, Hot Springs, Virginia.

Trout with Almond-Lemon Sauce courtesy of Mrs. Roger Waller, Birmingham, Alabama.

Virginia Baked Scallops adapted from *Southern Scope* by The Virginia Seafood Industry, Newport News, Virginia.

INDEX